Floral Mandala

Coloring Book

Mandala Wonderland Series
Volume # 2

This Book Belongs To:

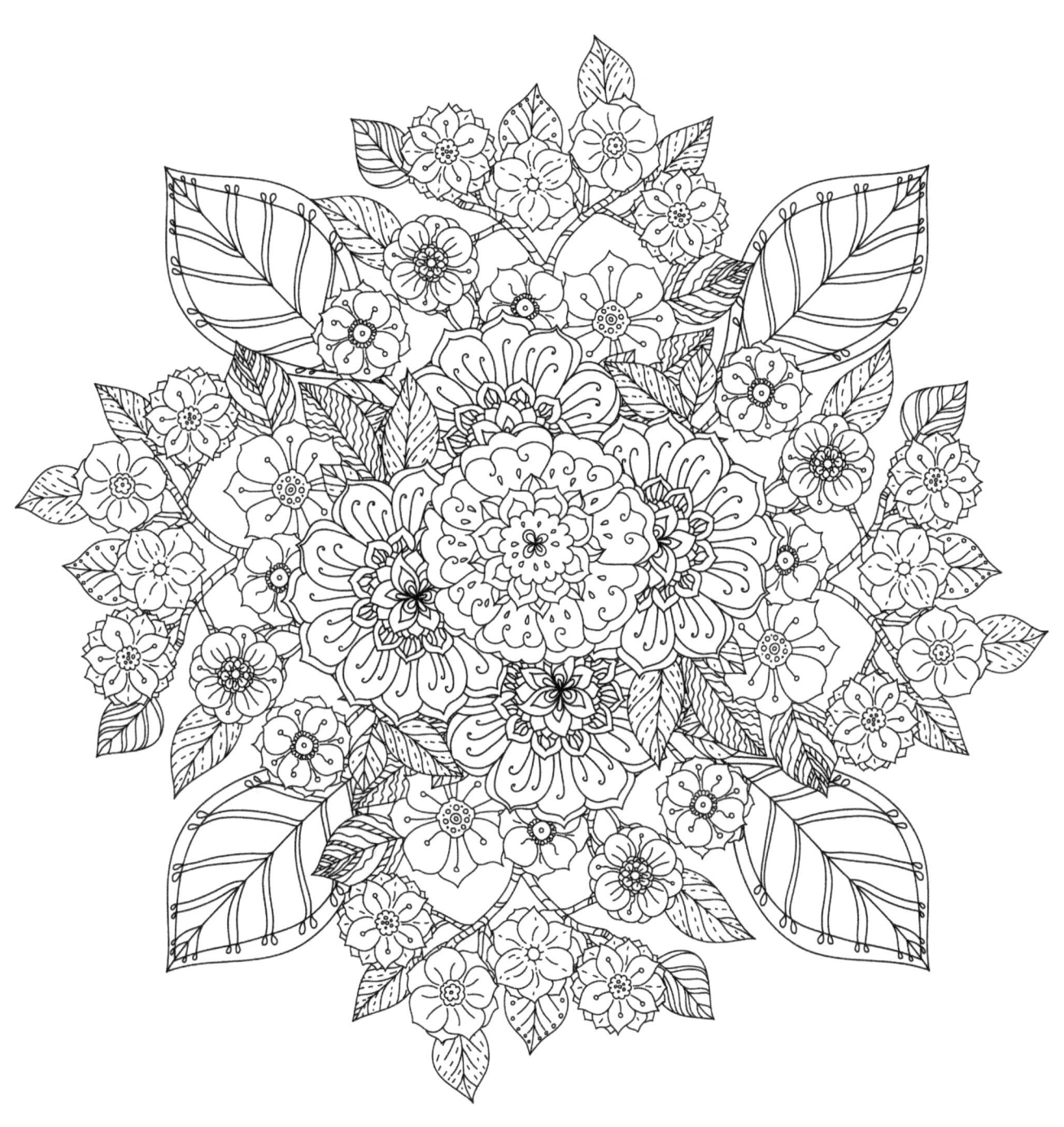

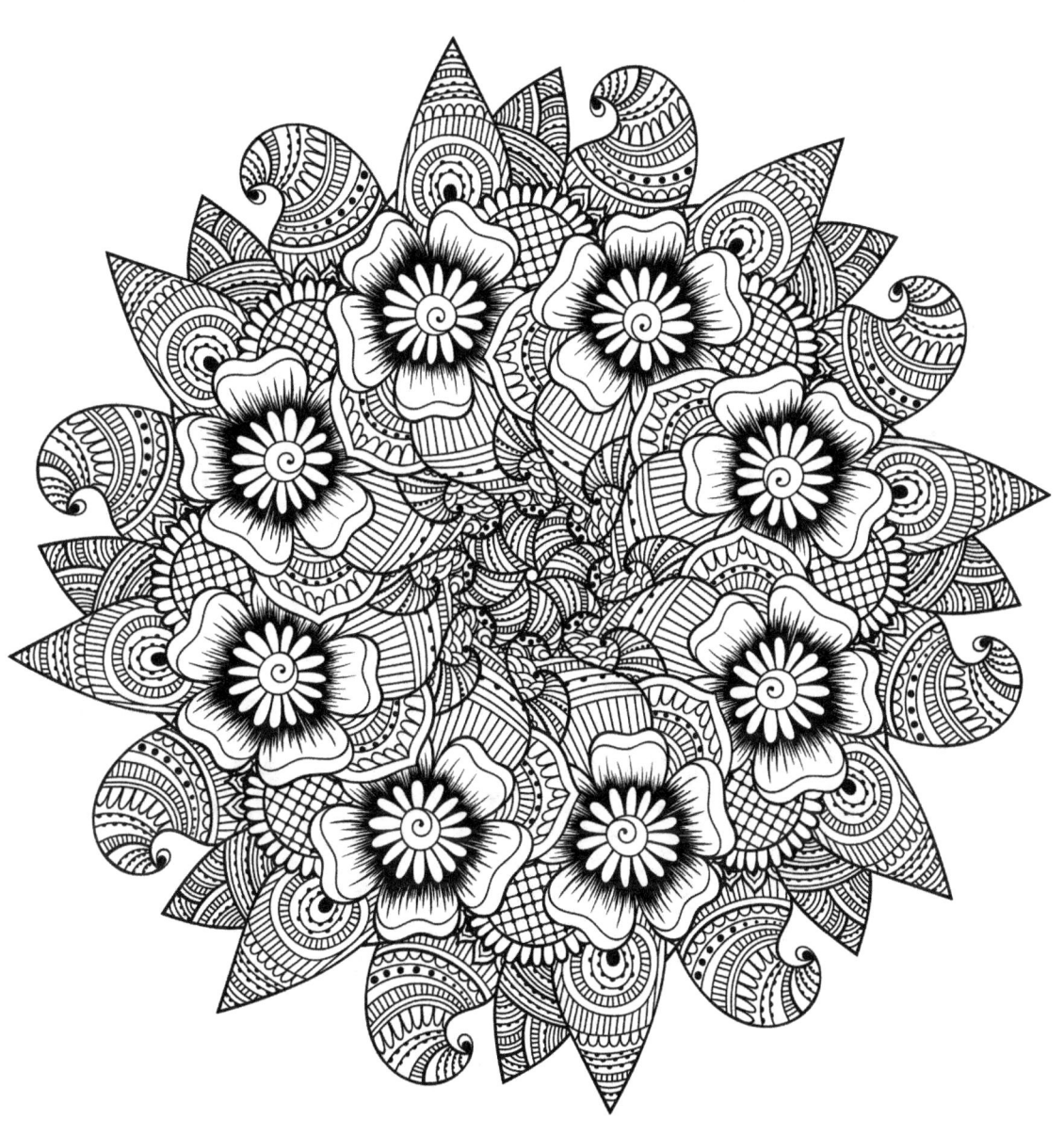

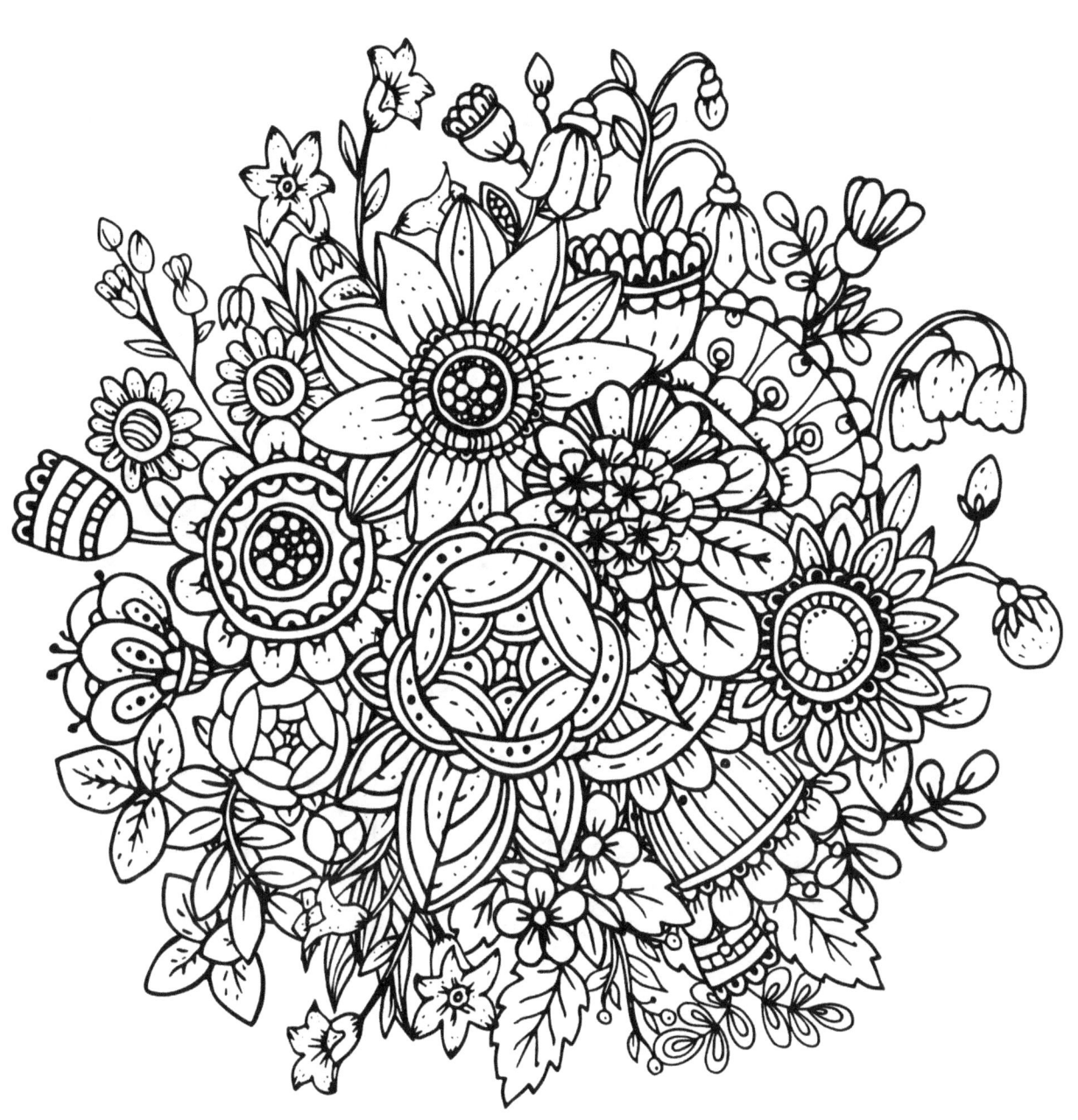

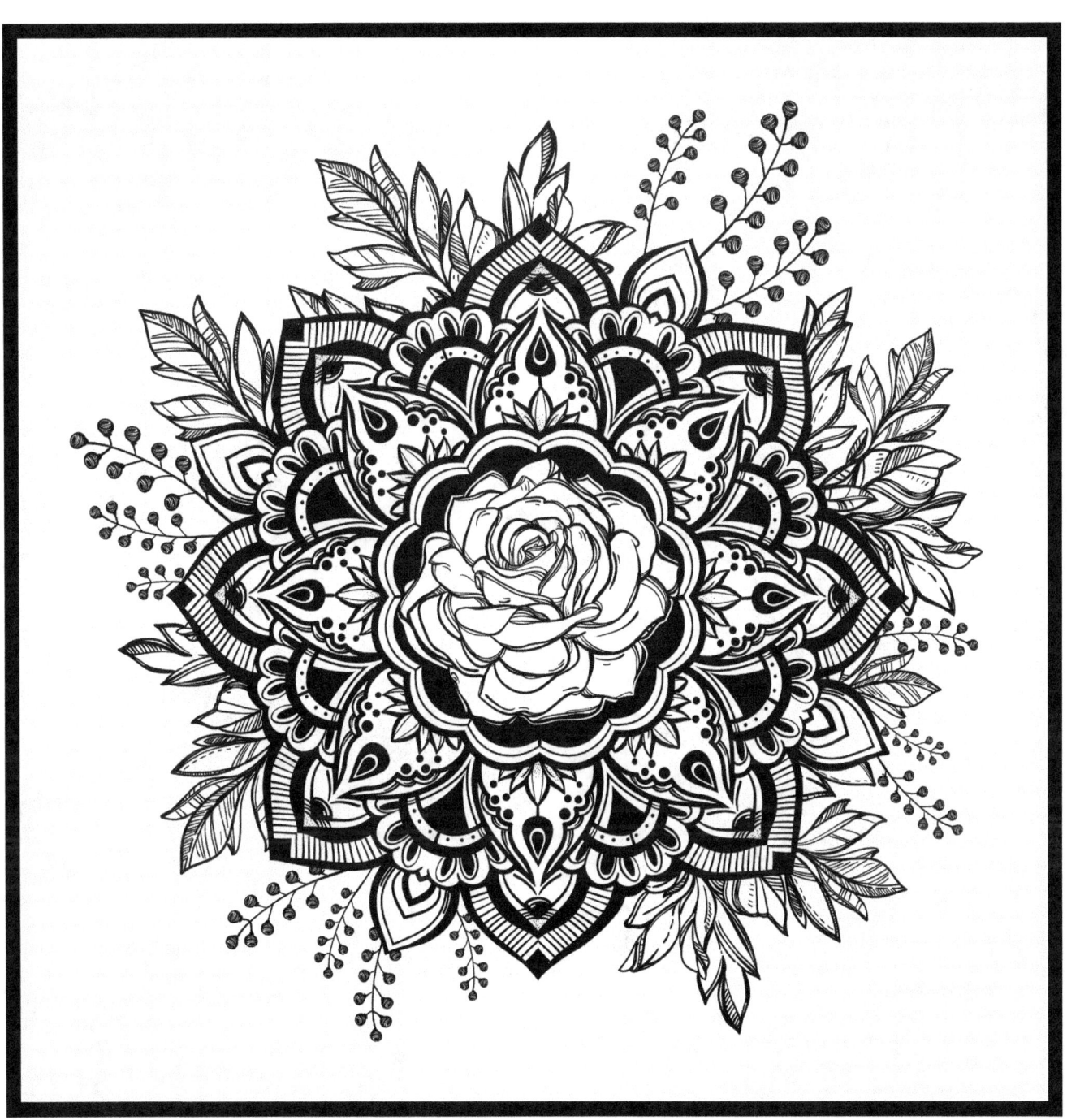

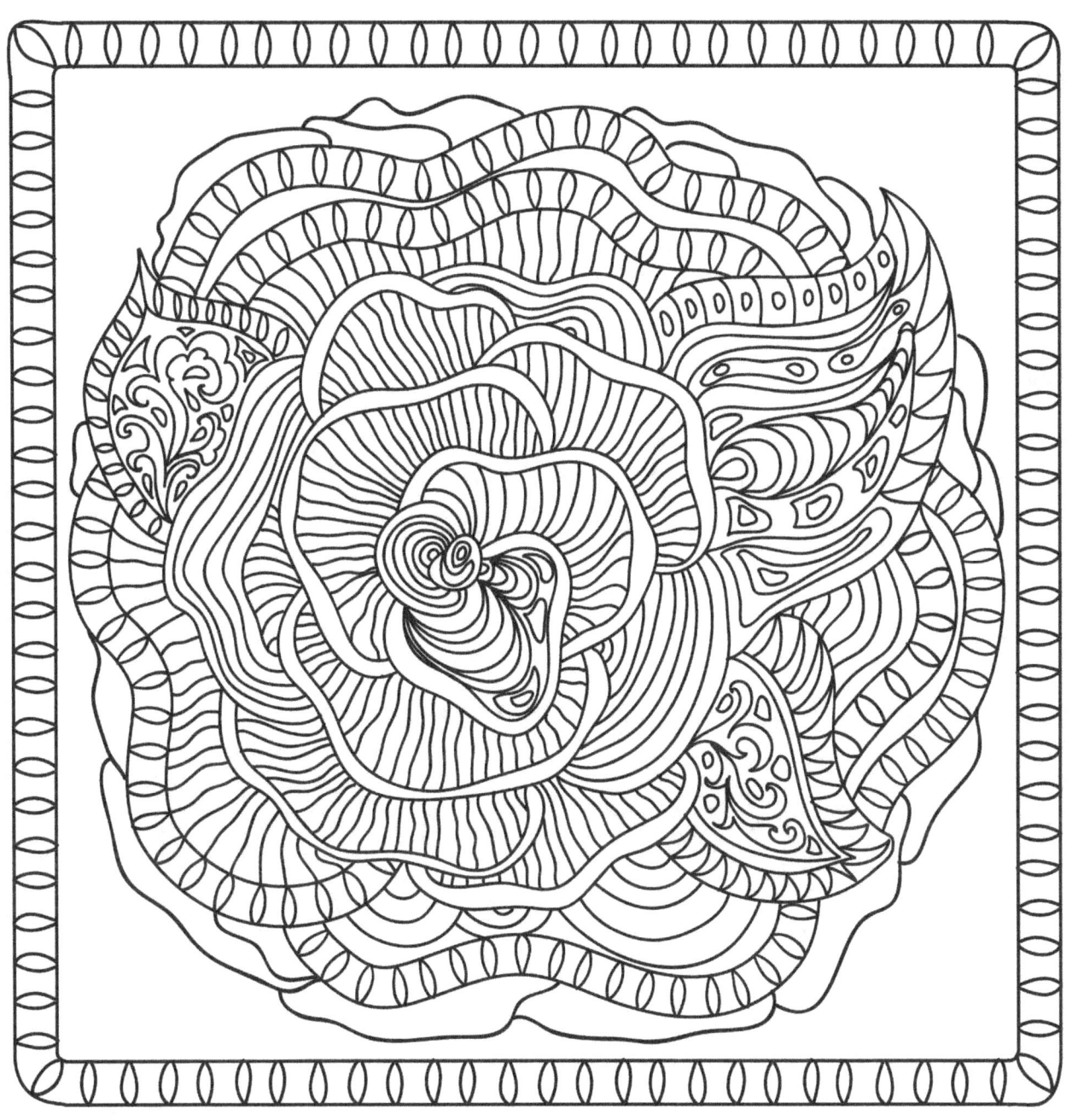

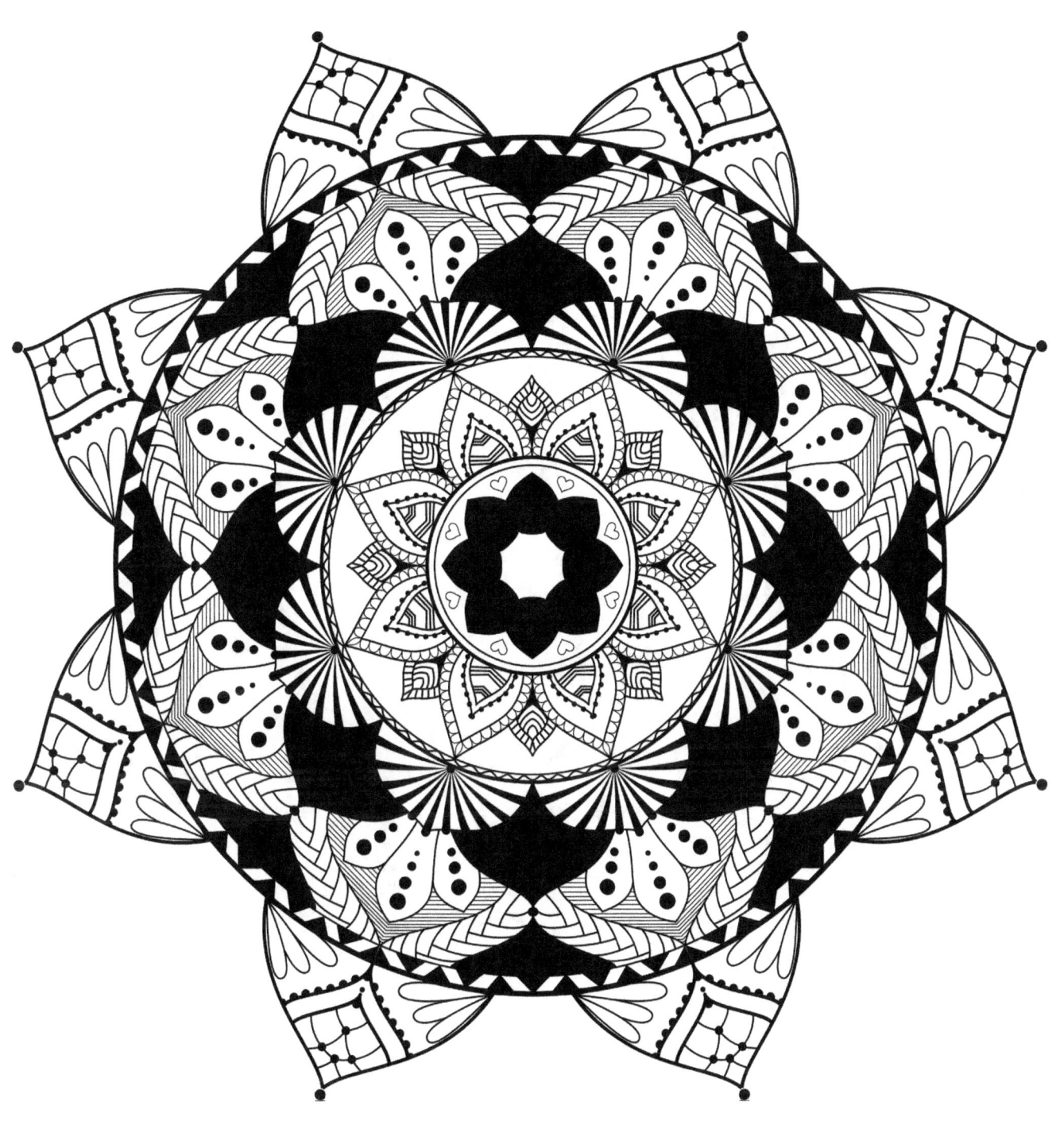

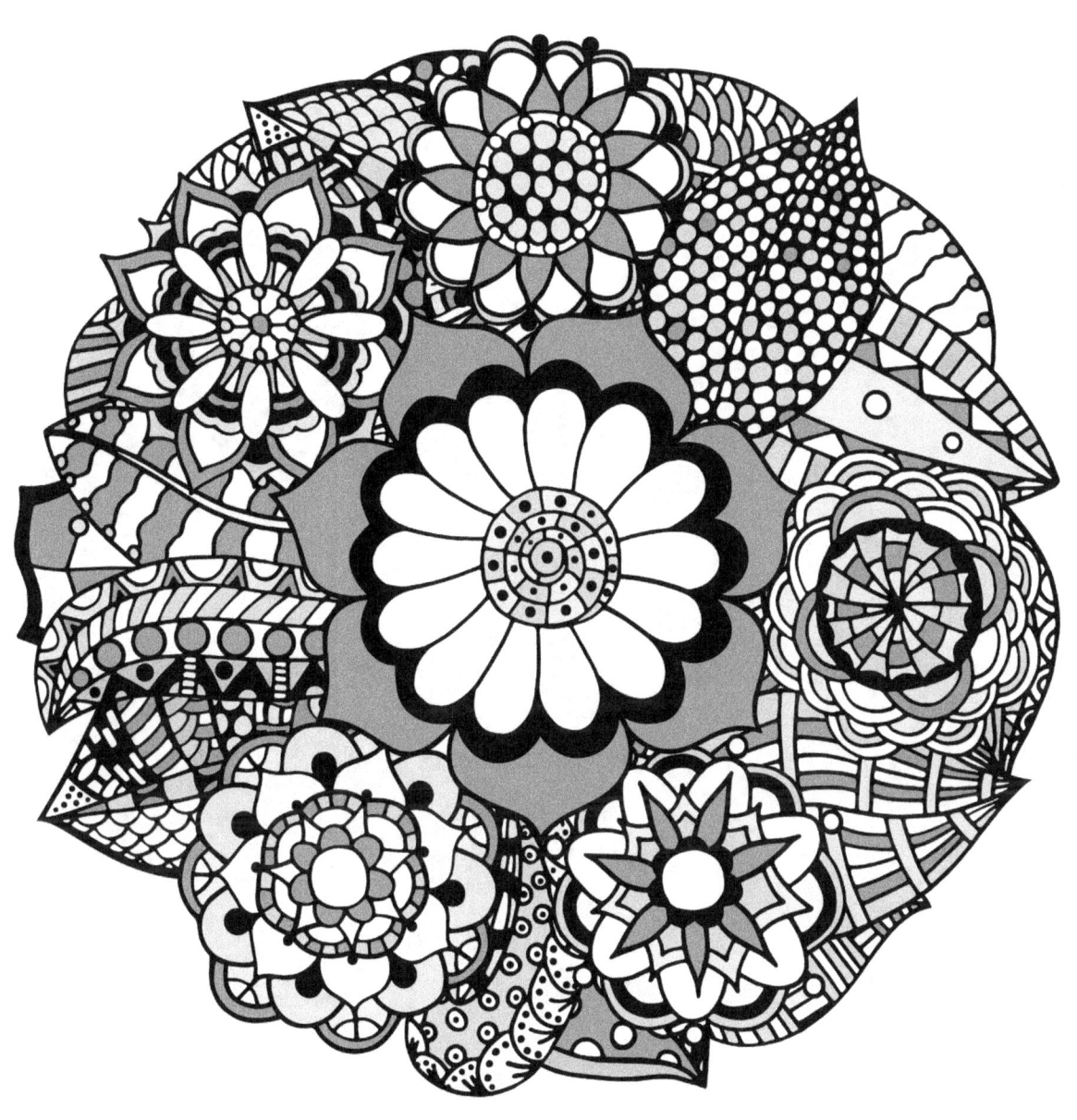

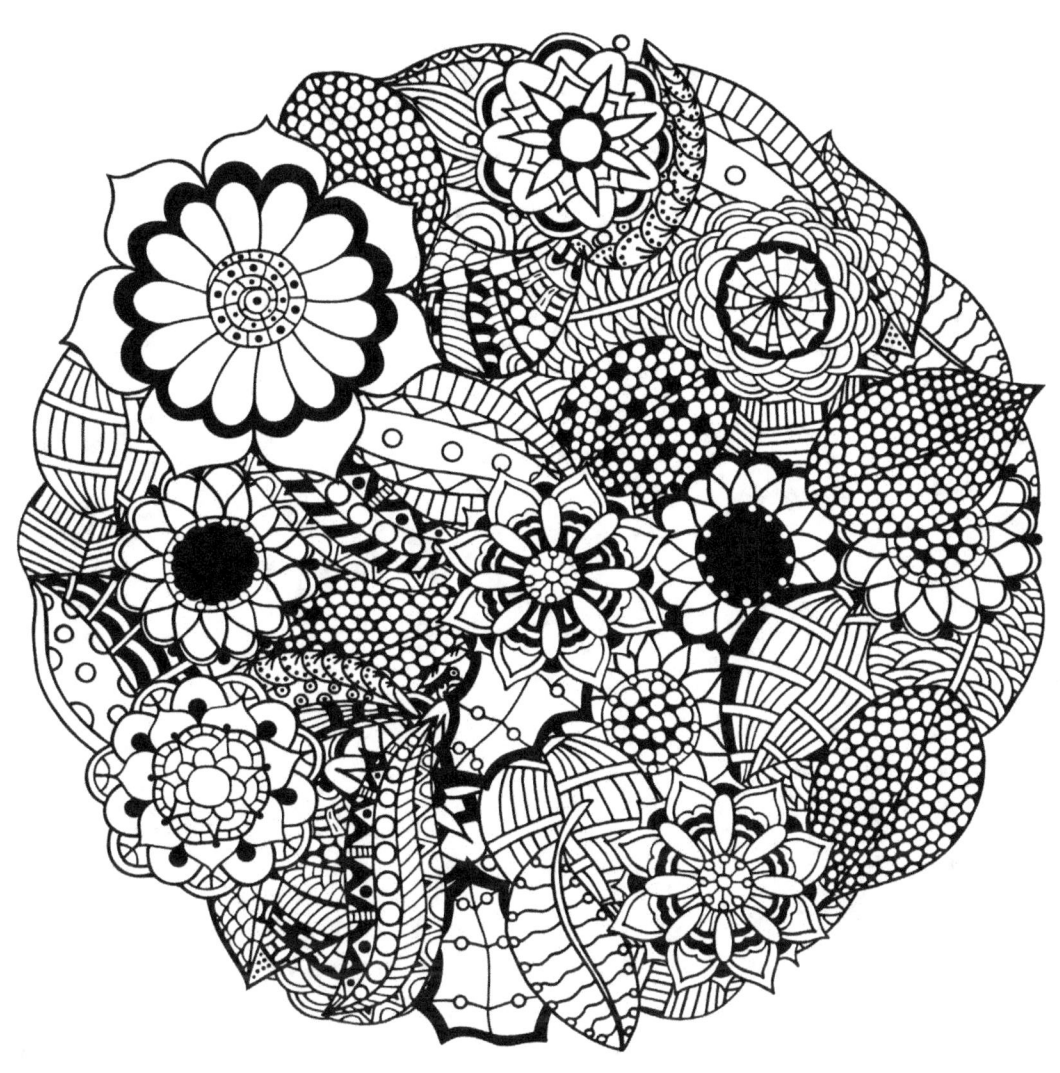

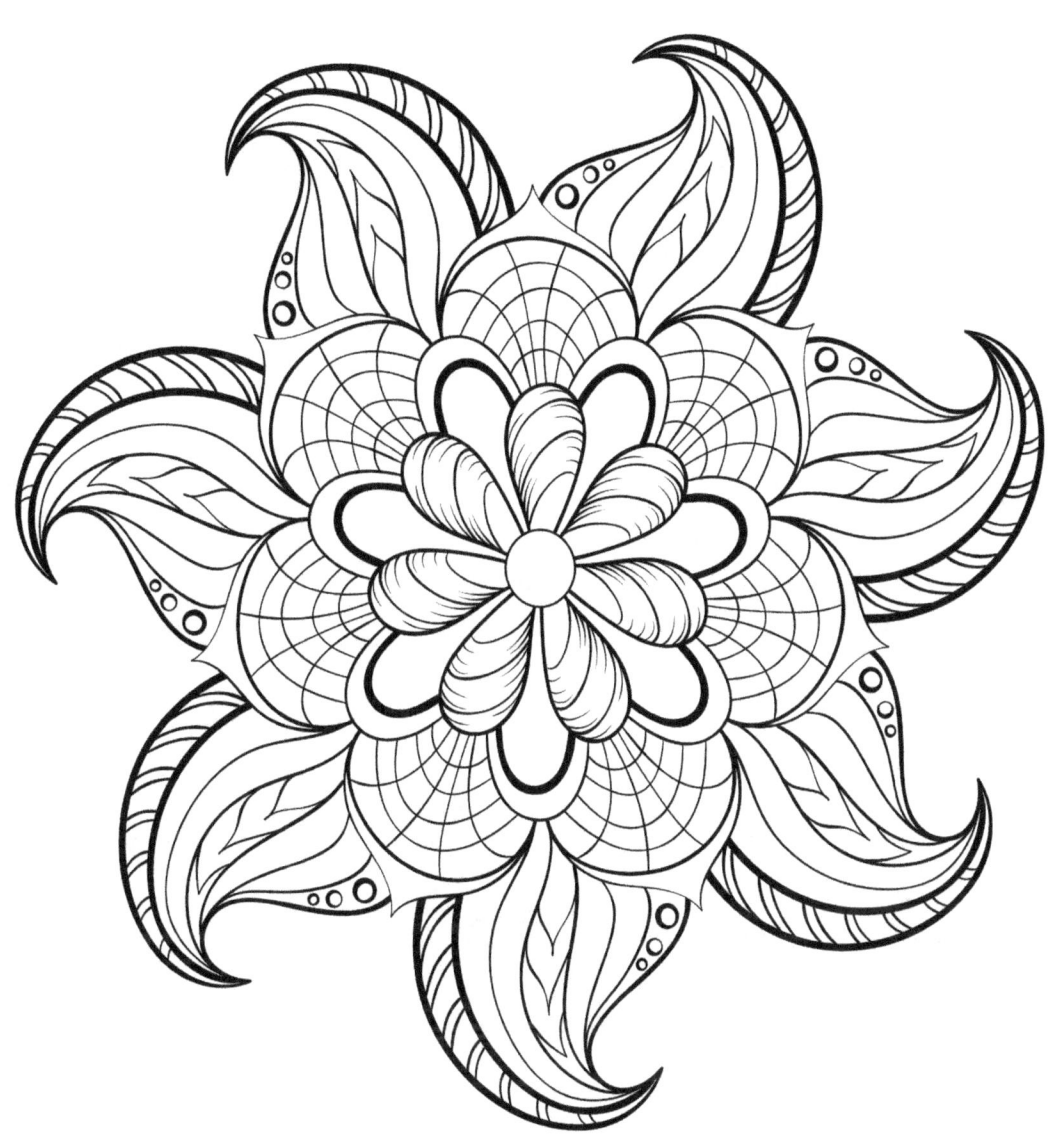

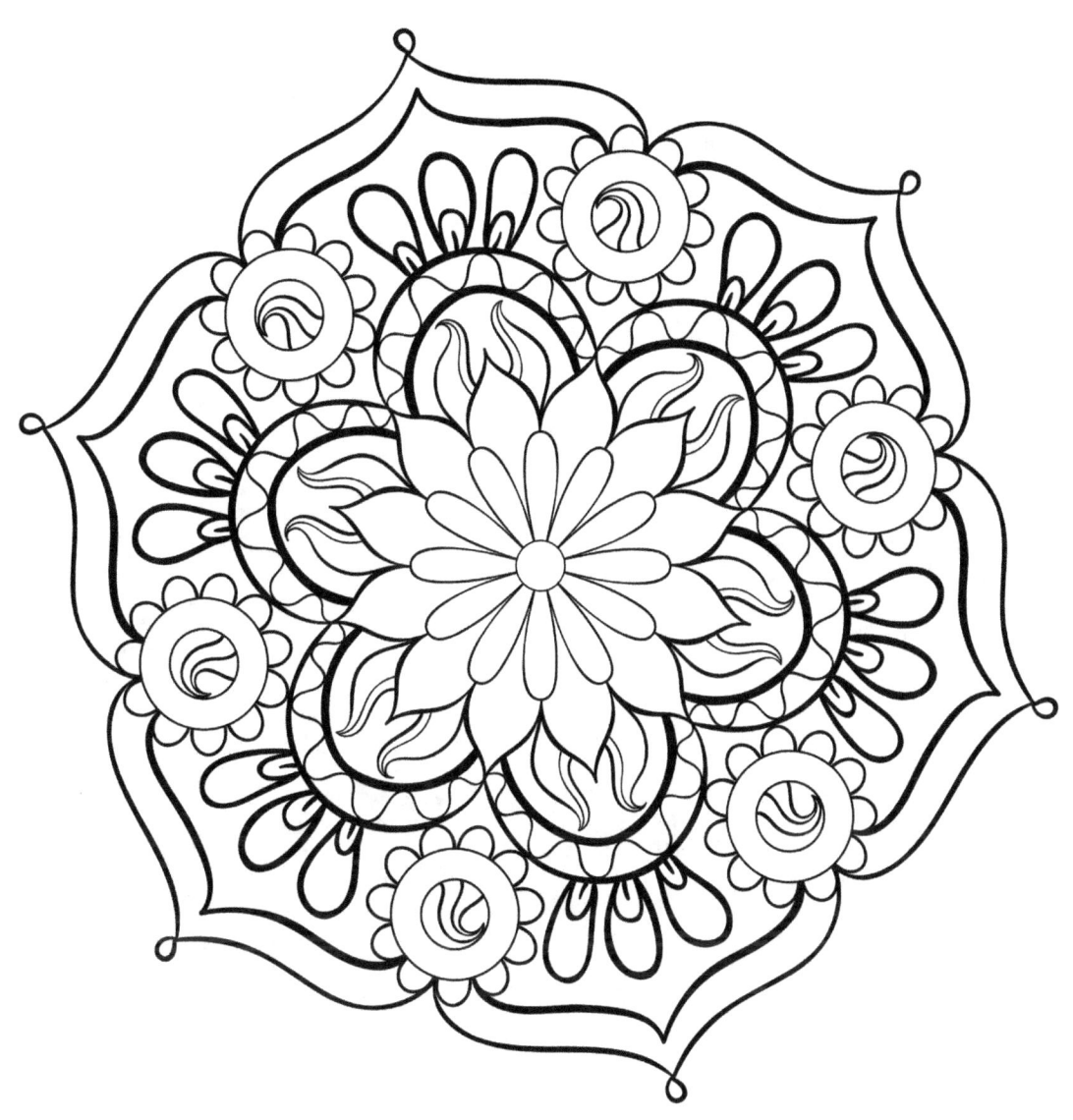

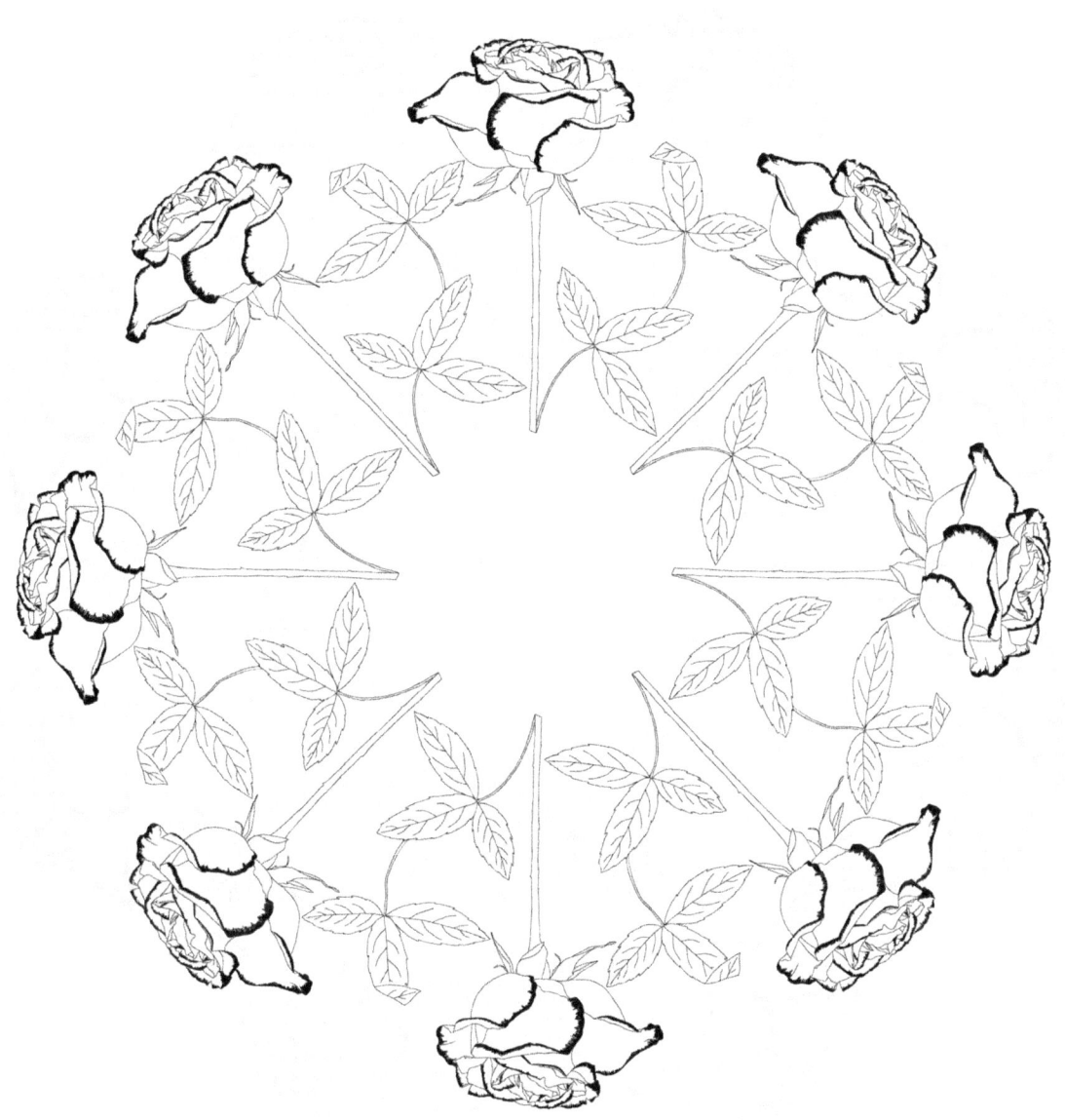

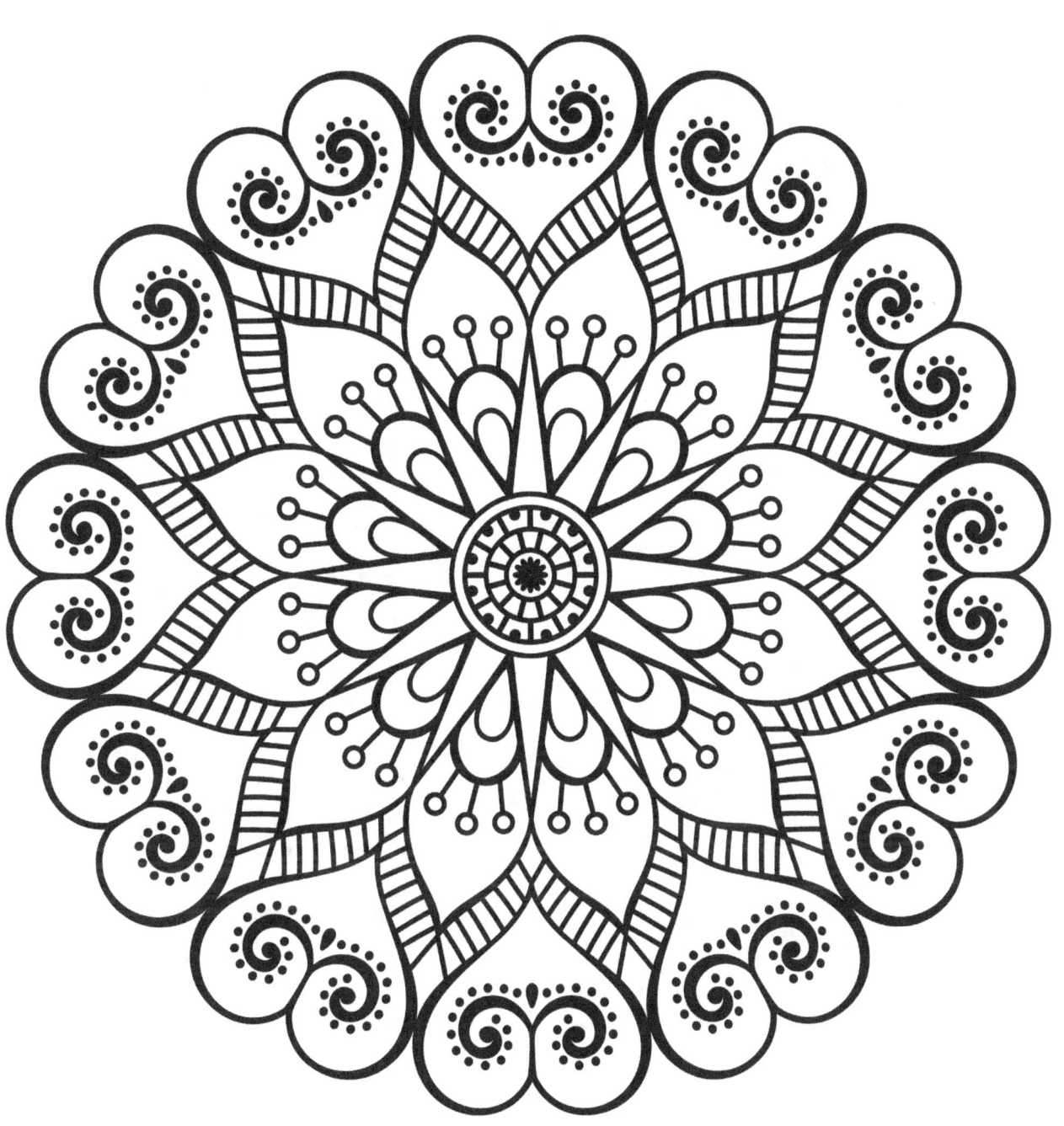

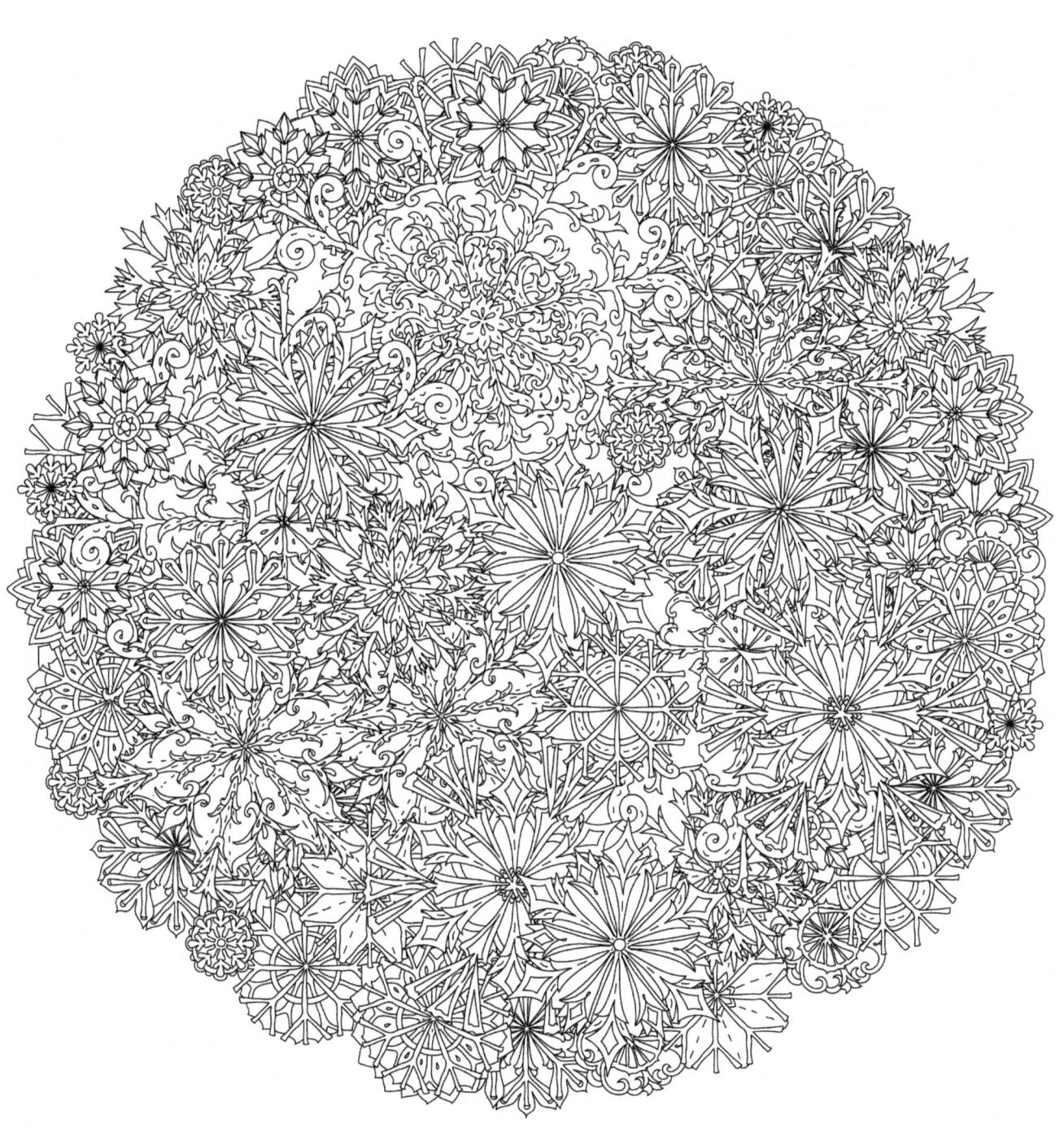

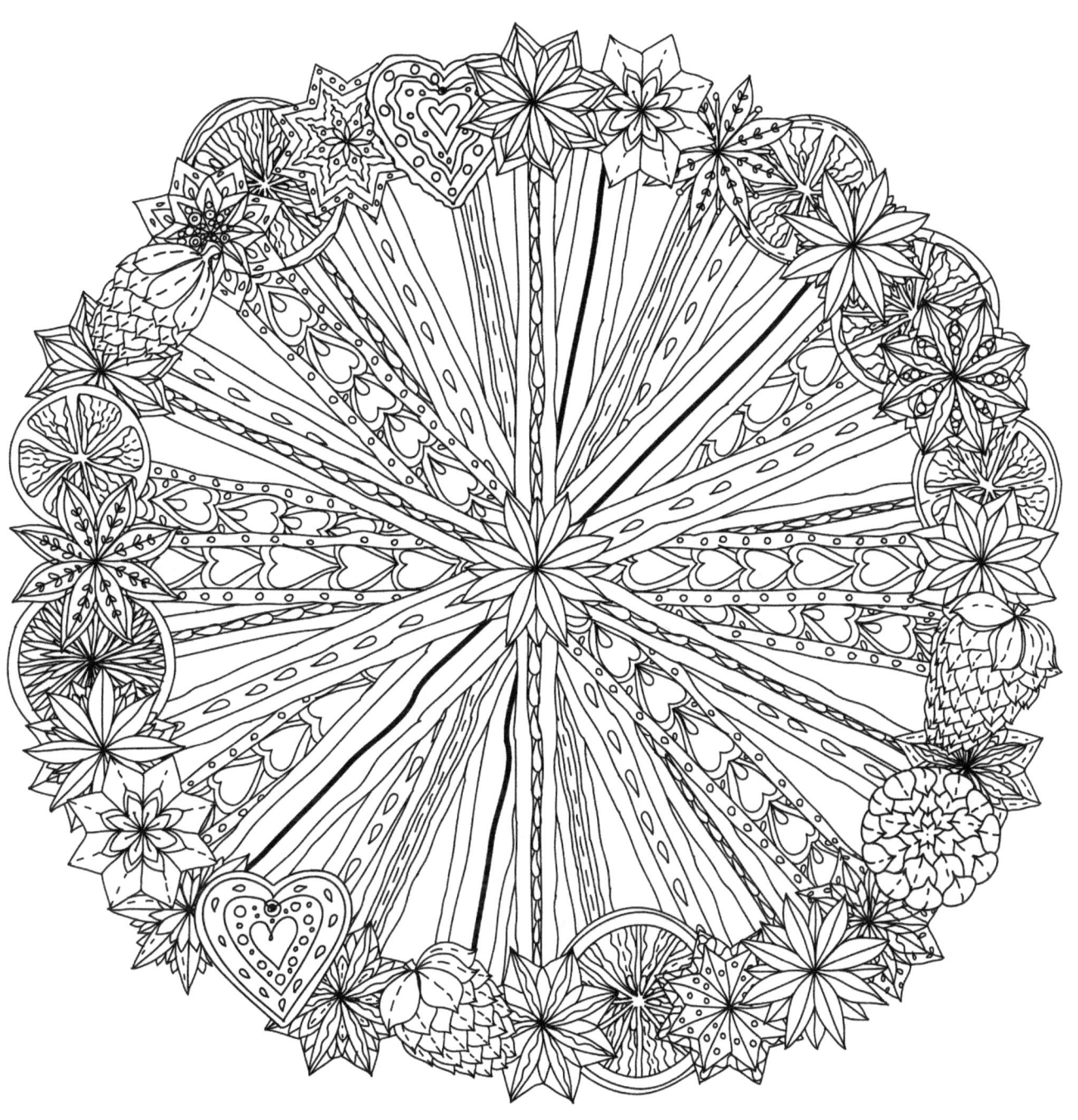

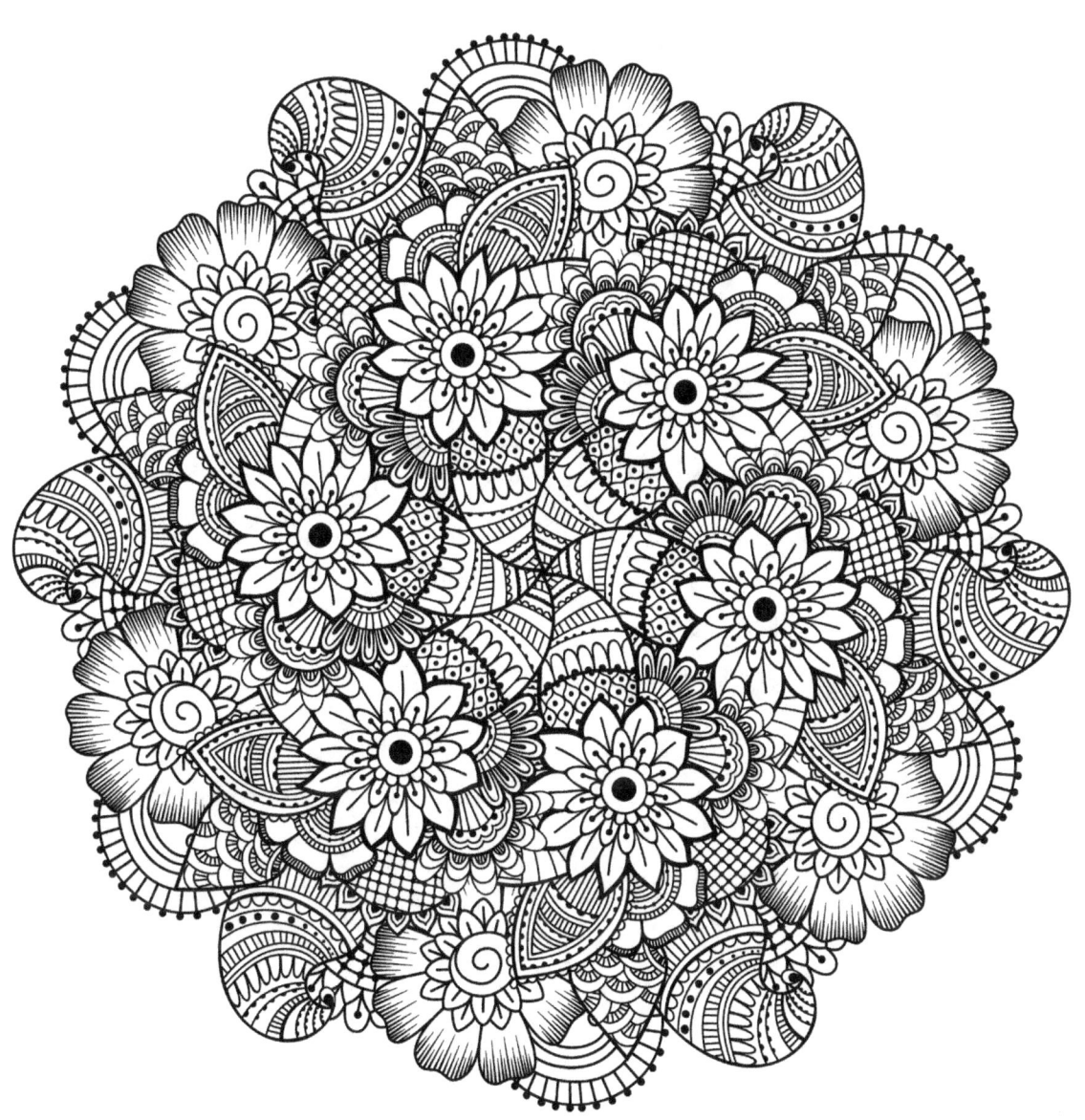

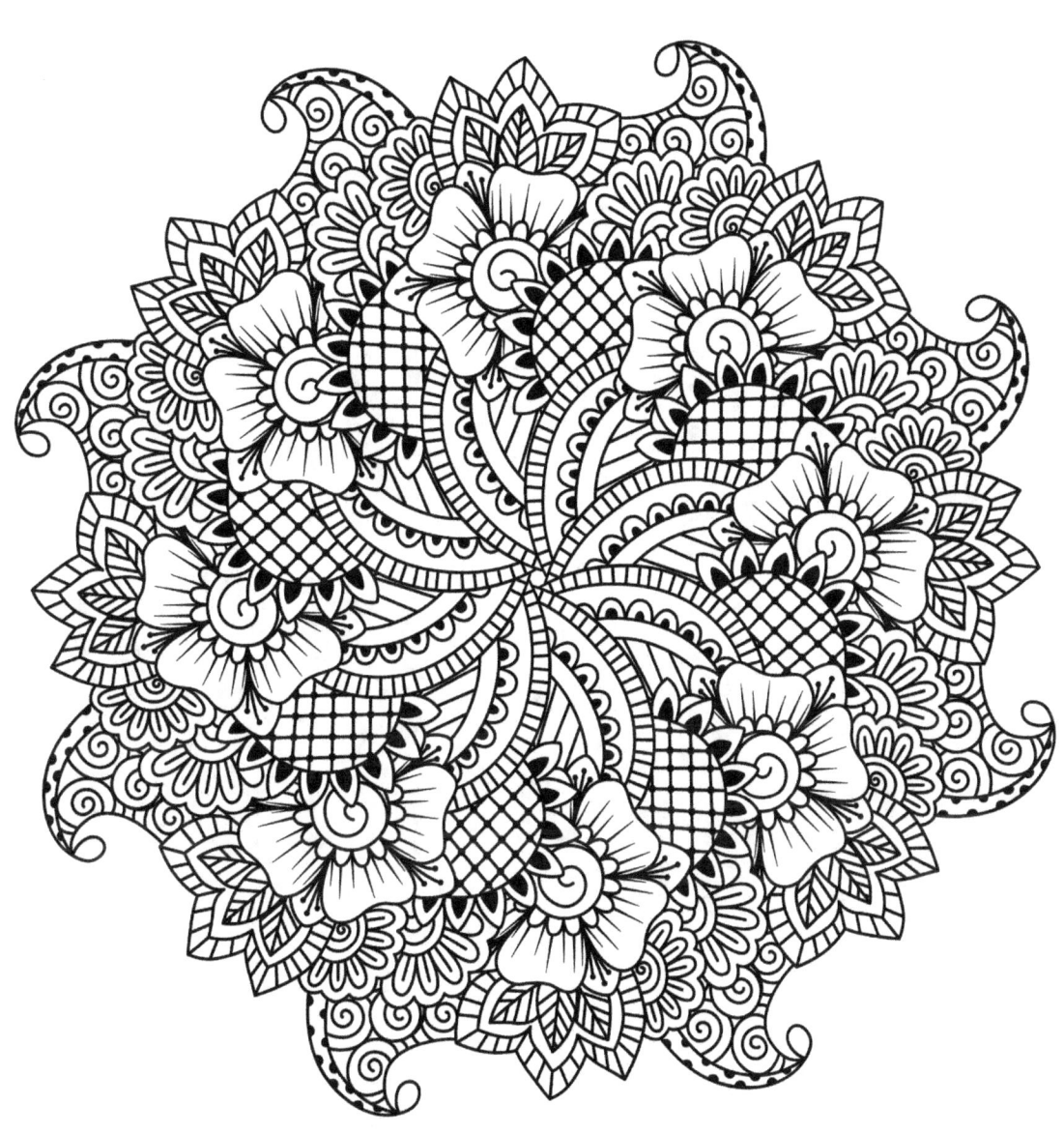

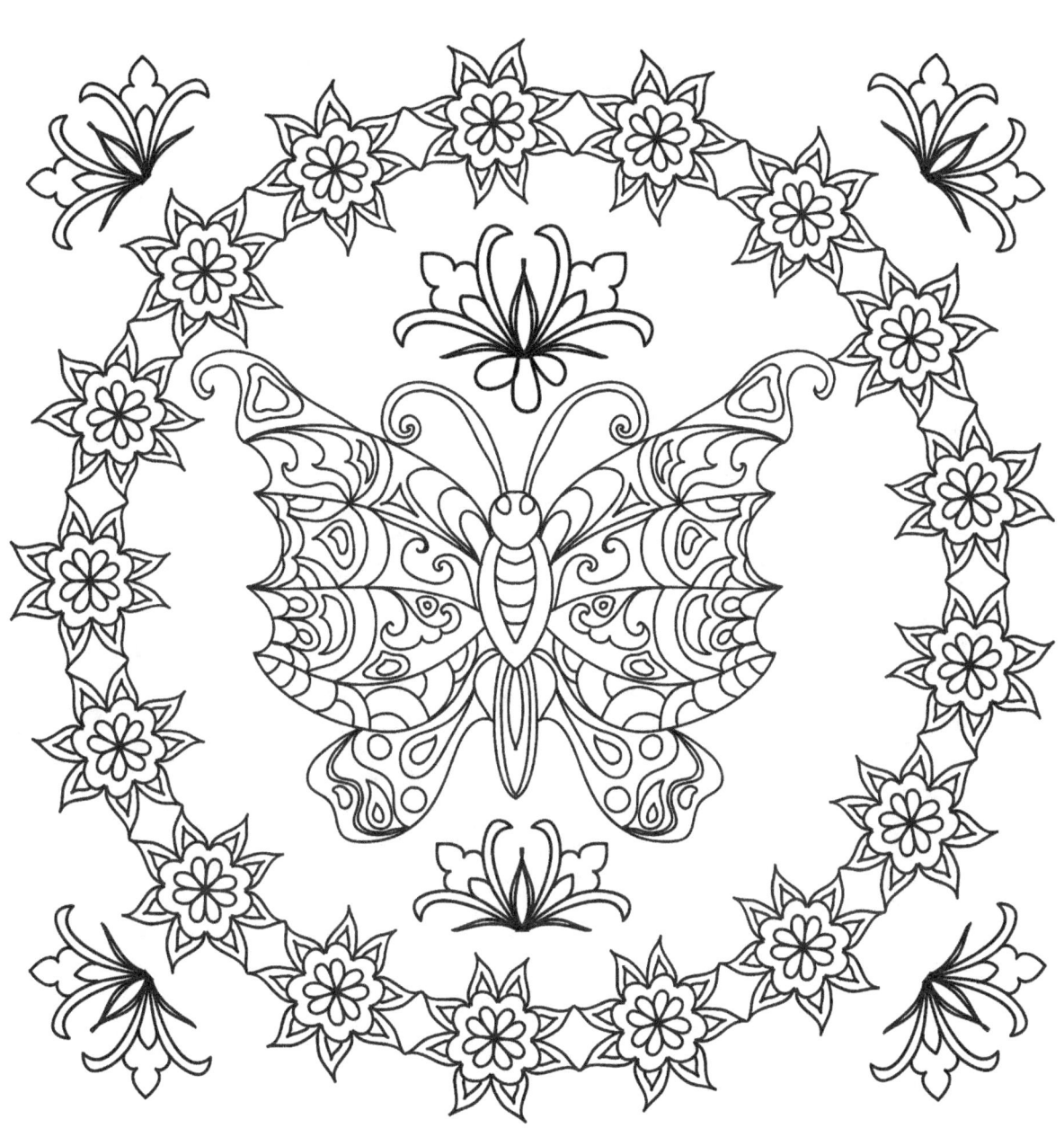

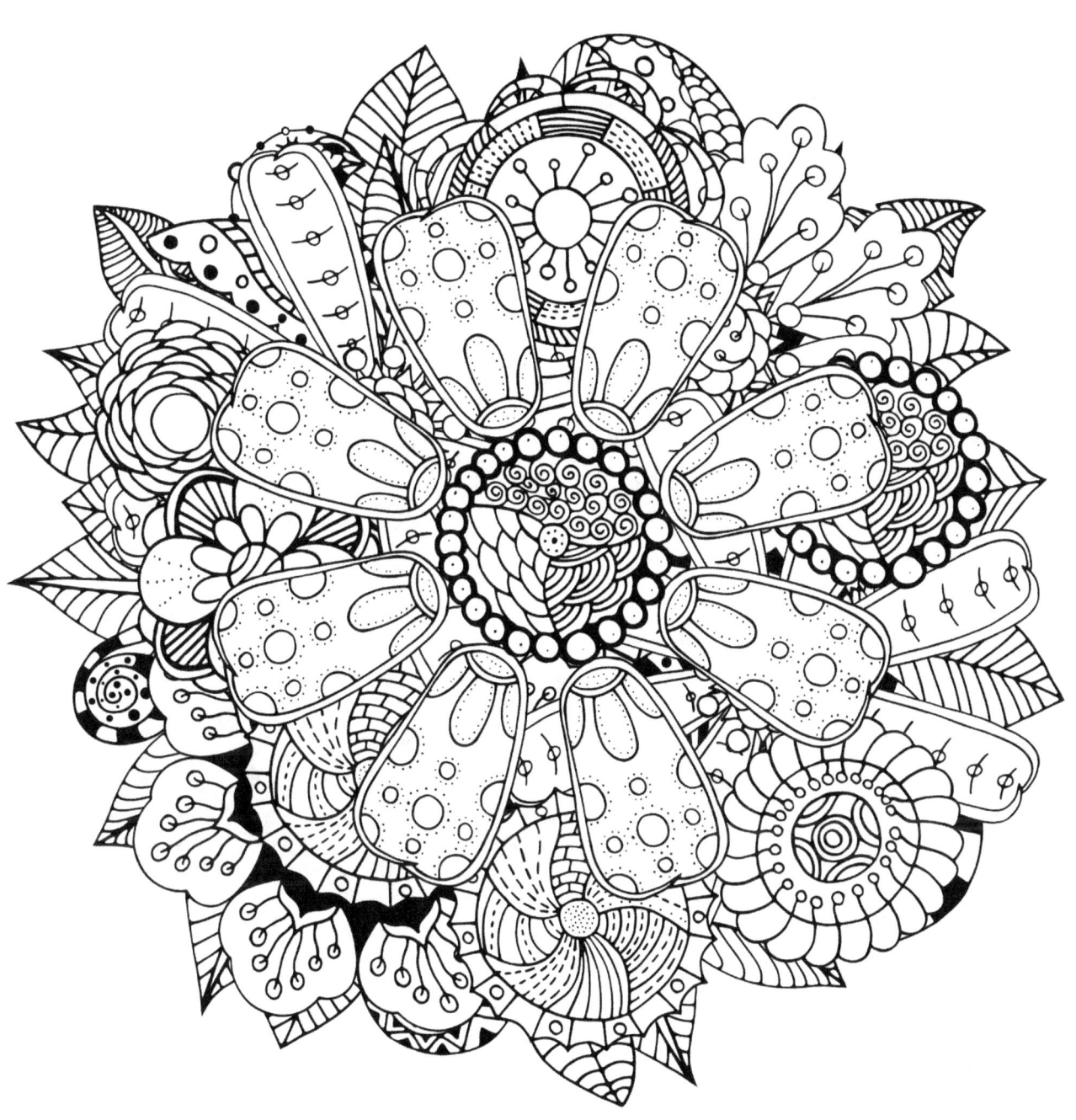

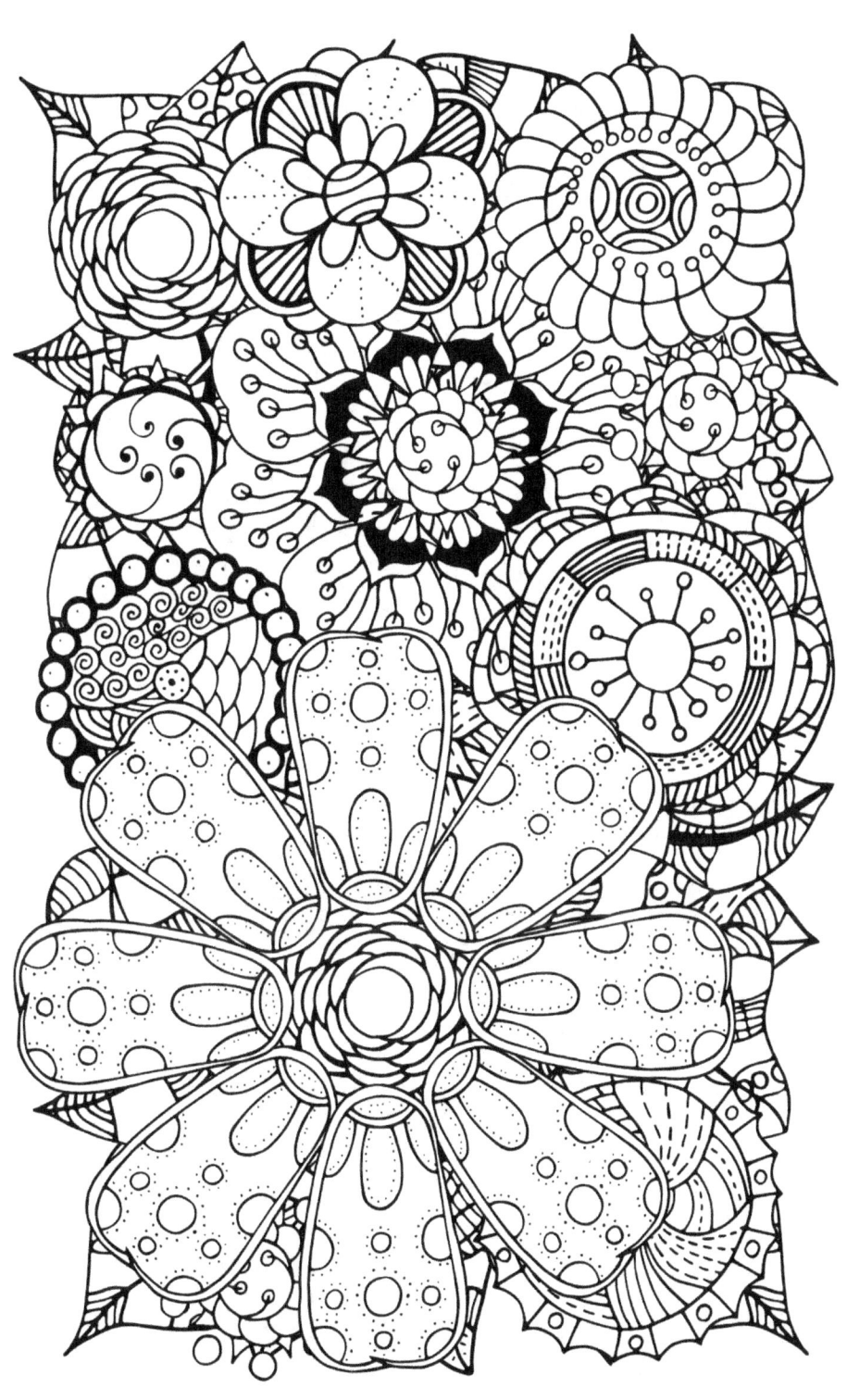

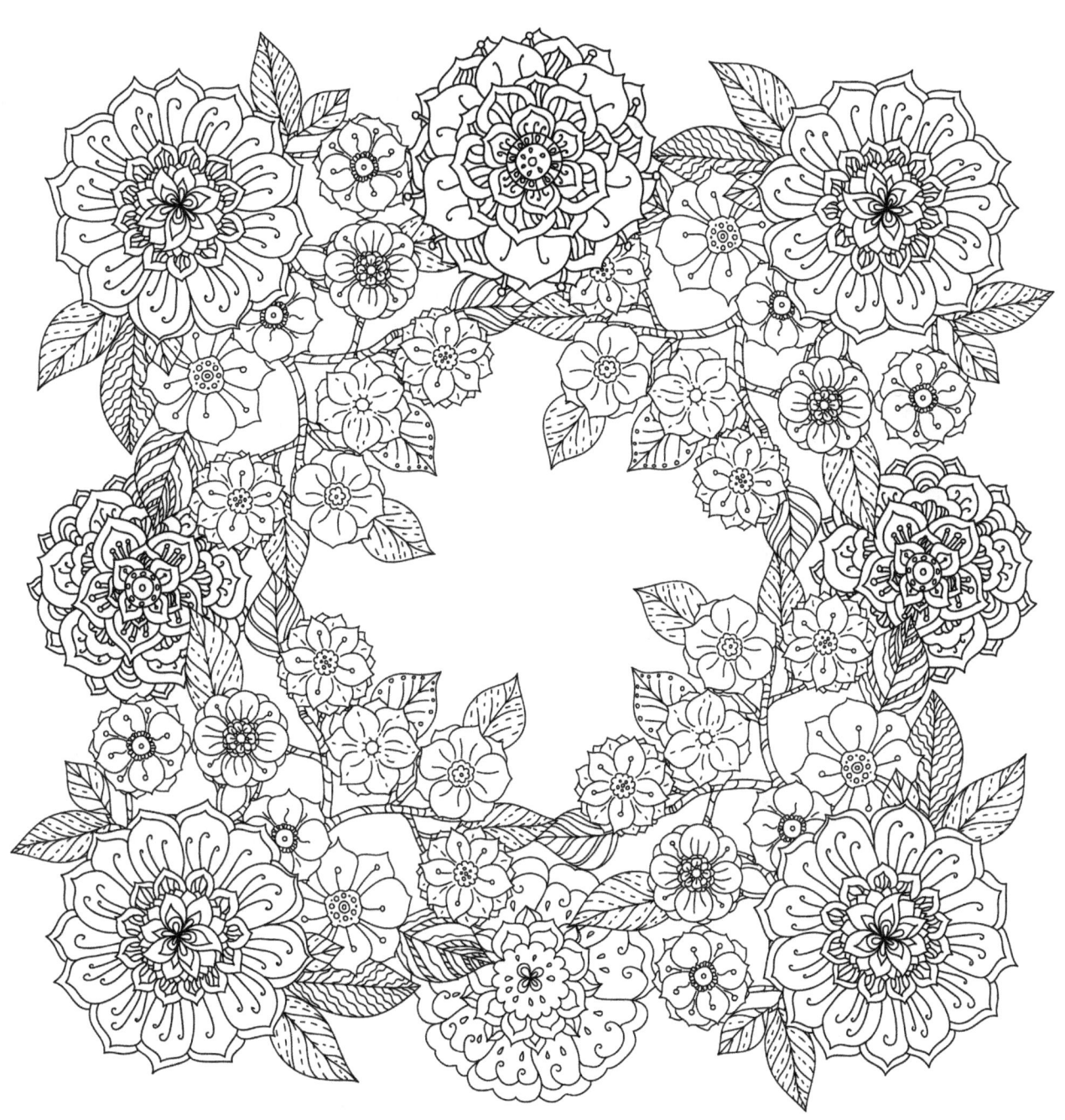

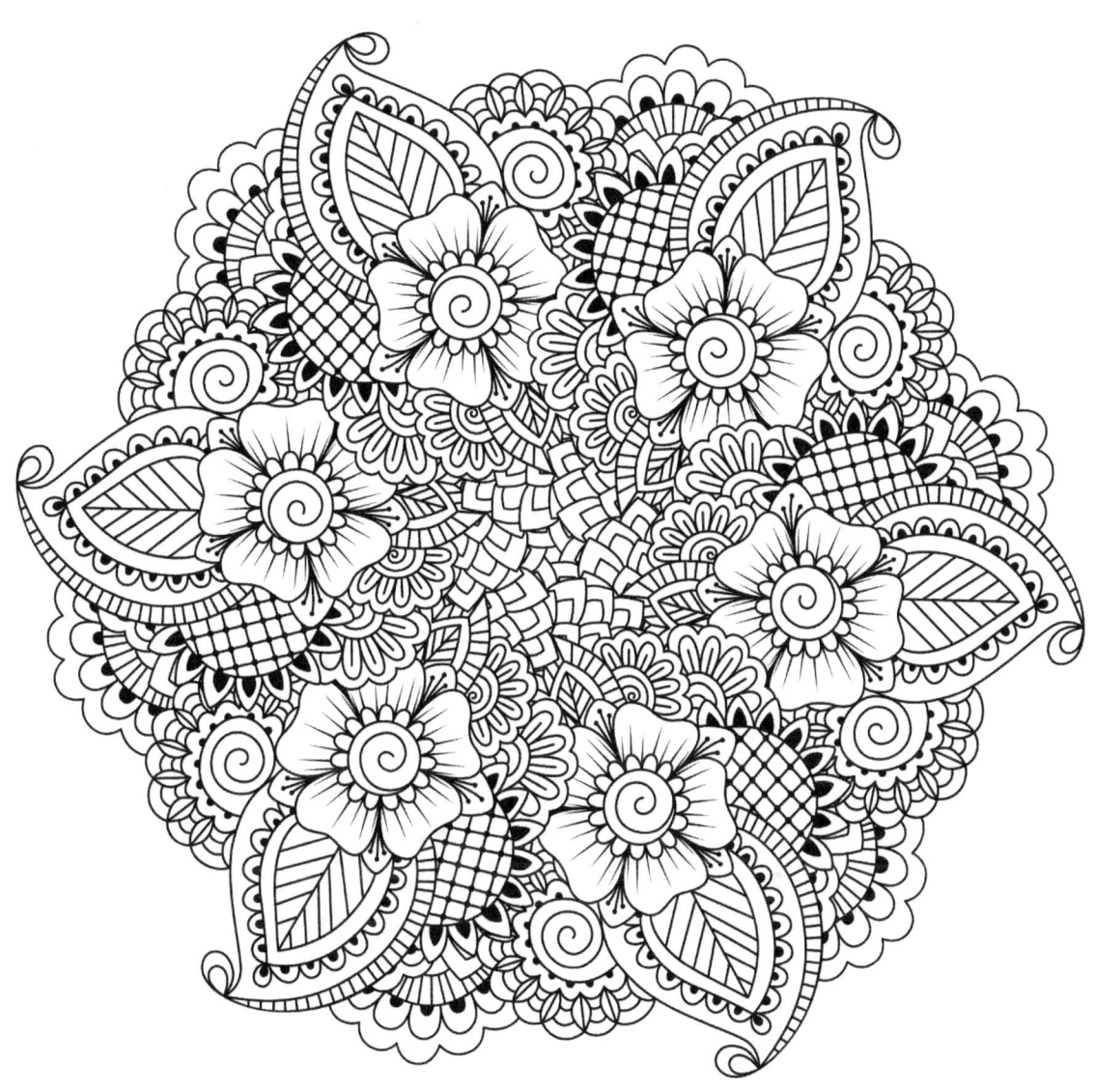

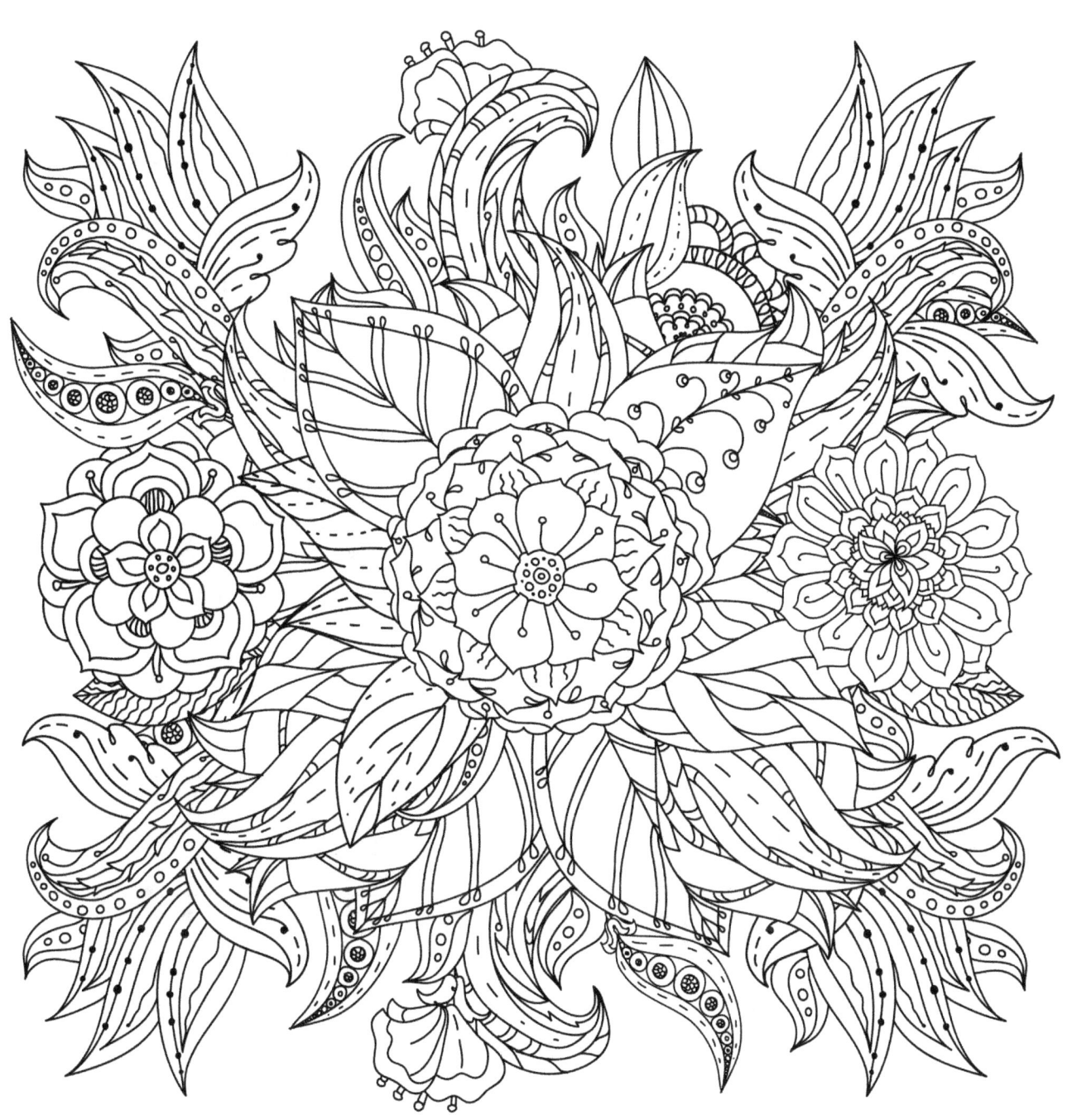

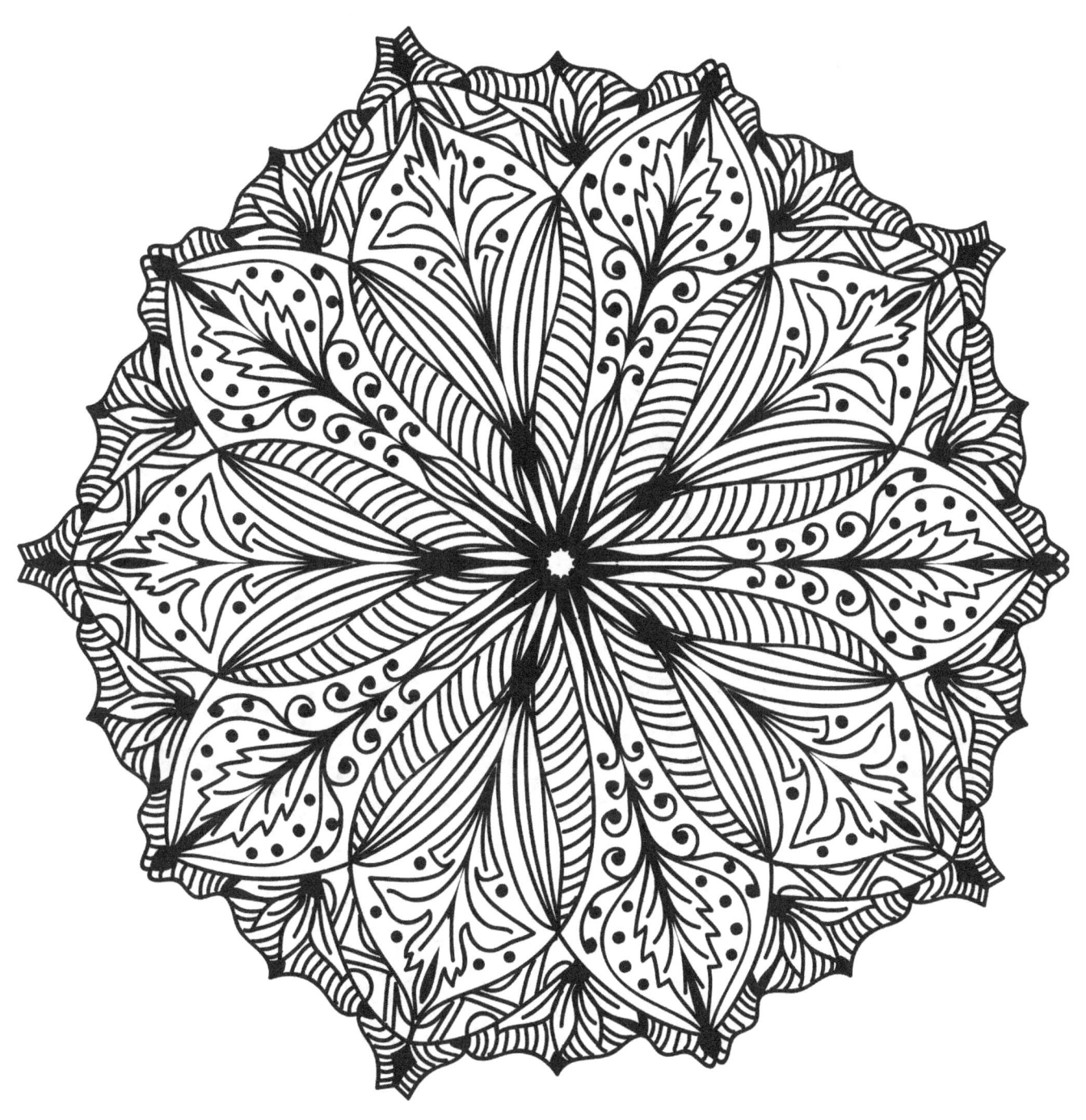

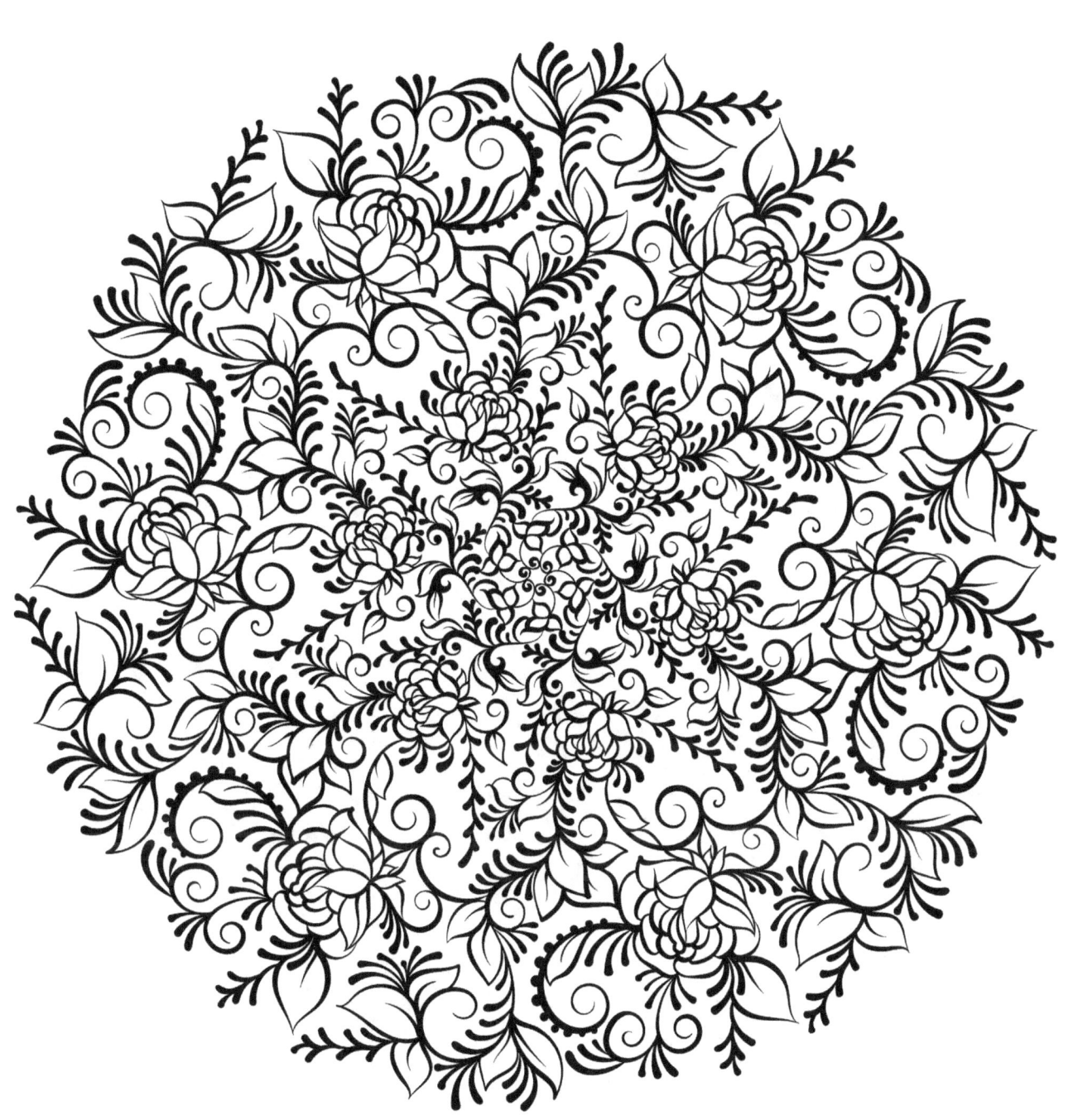

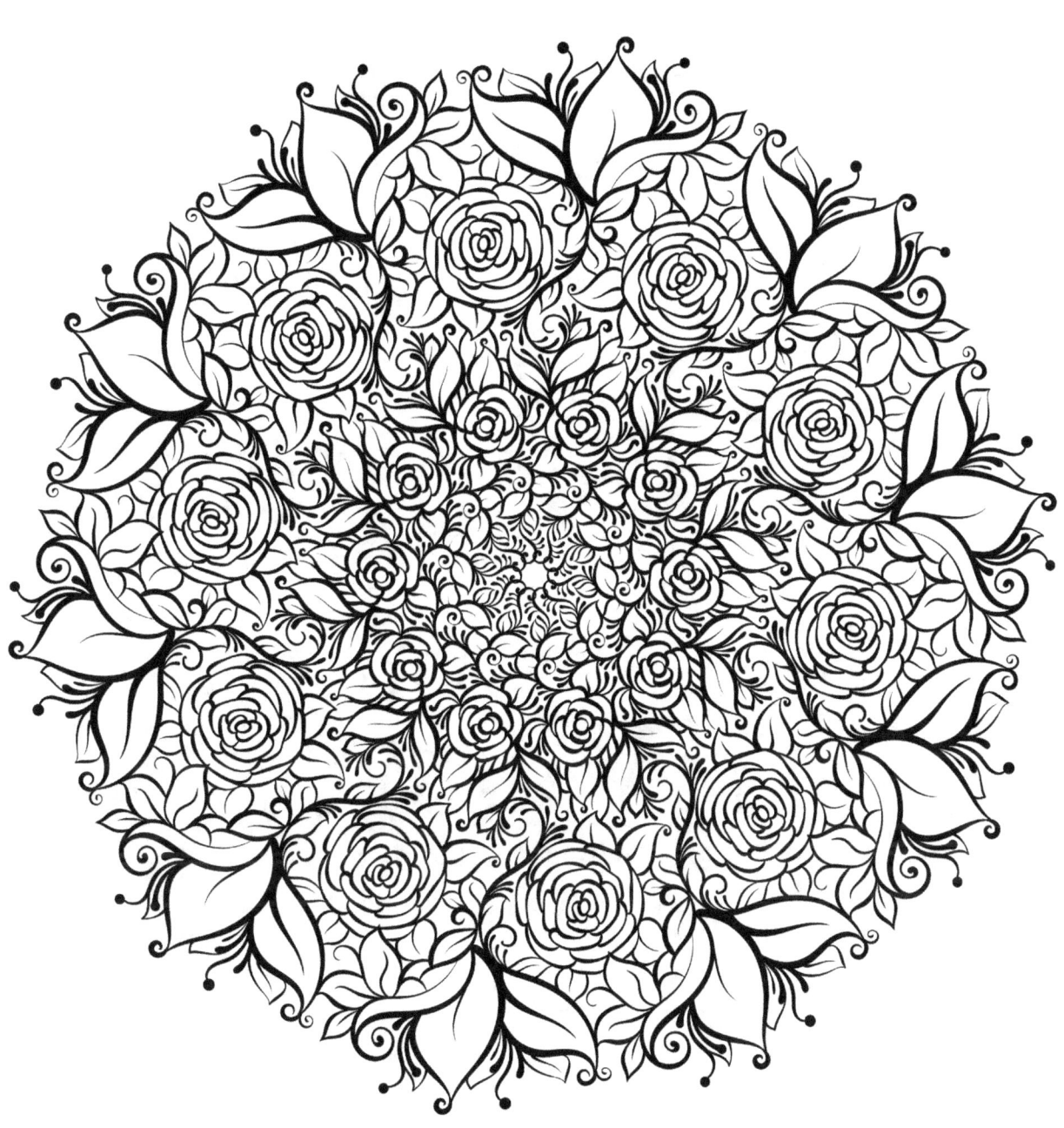

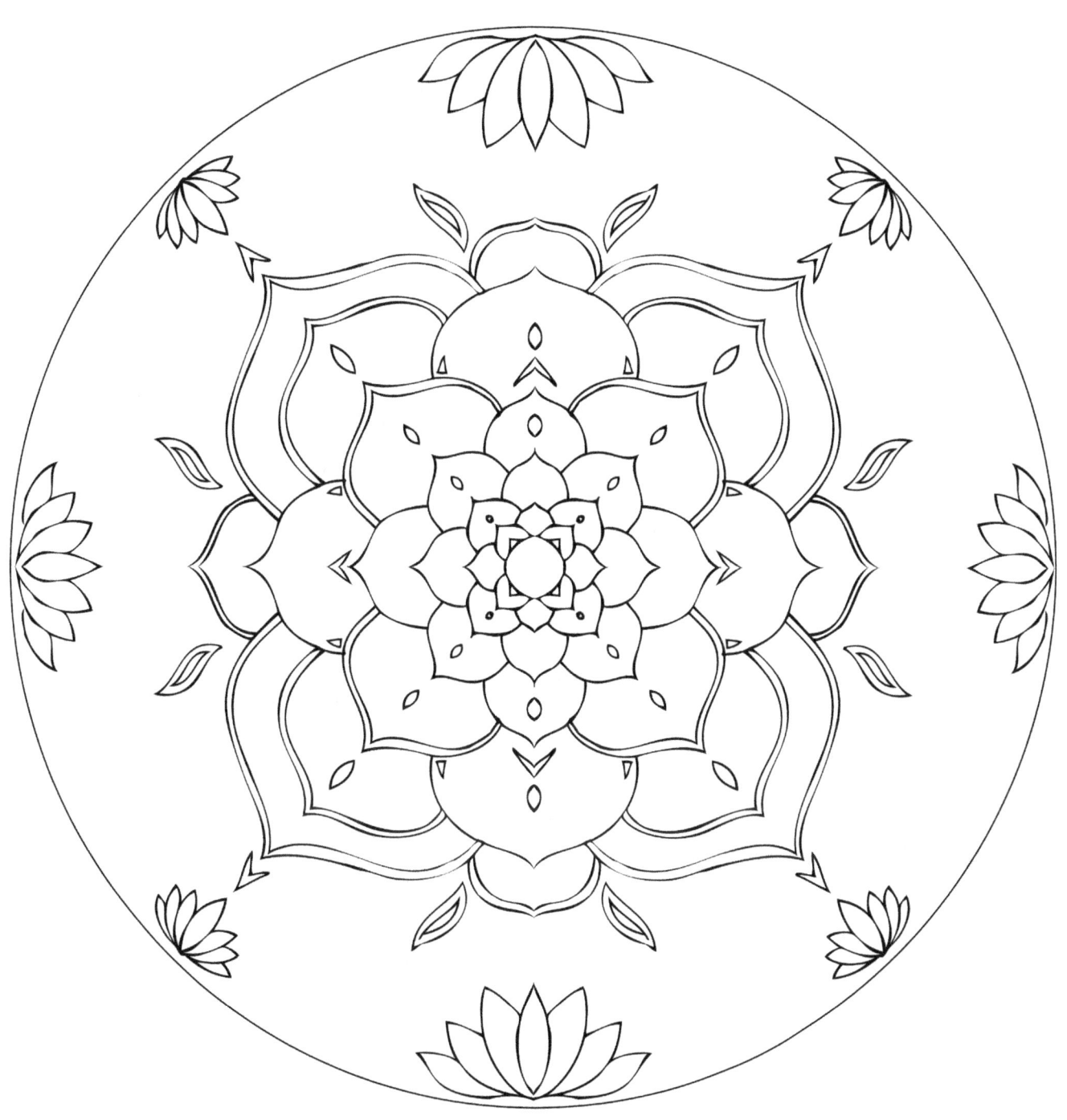

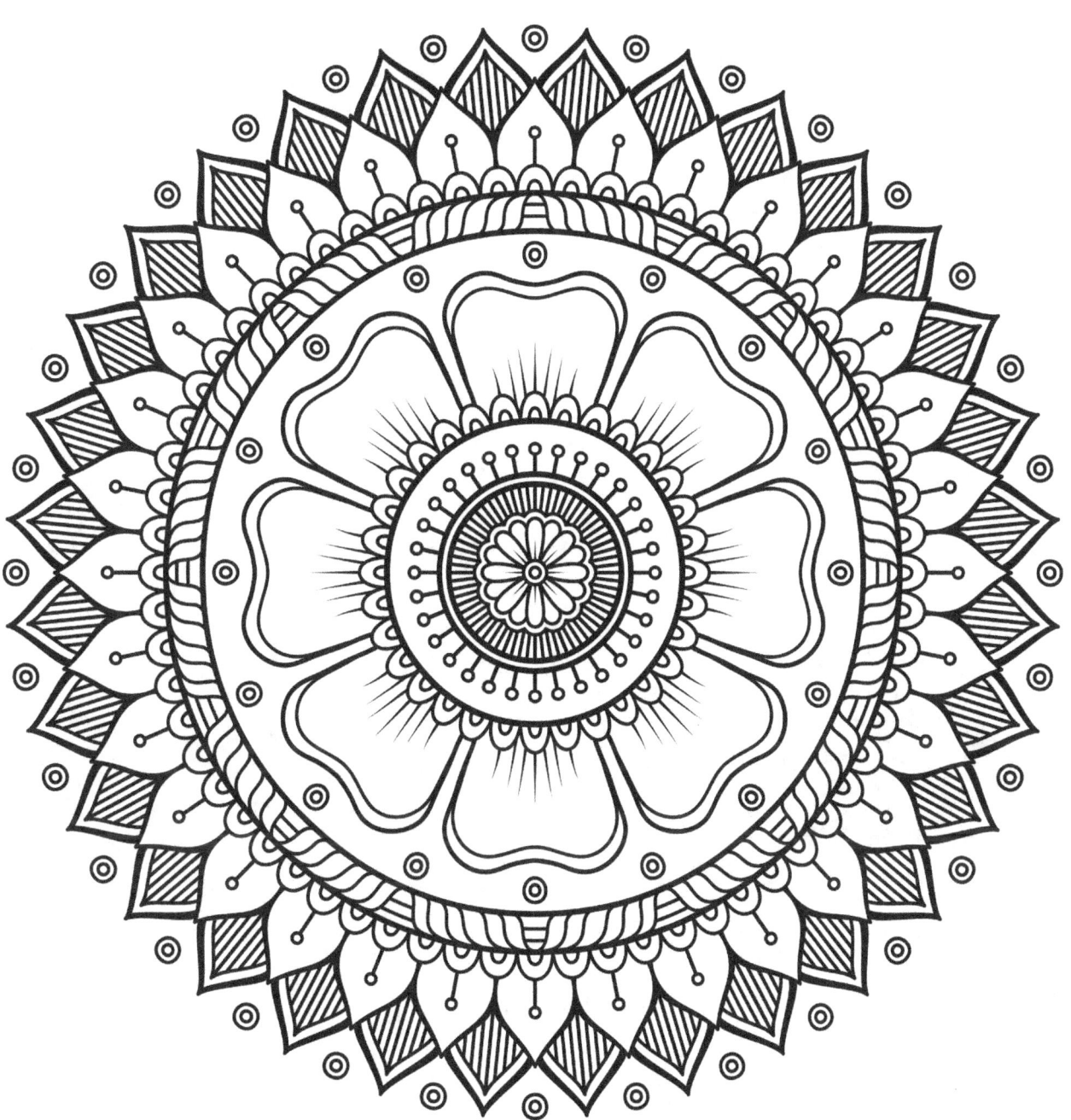

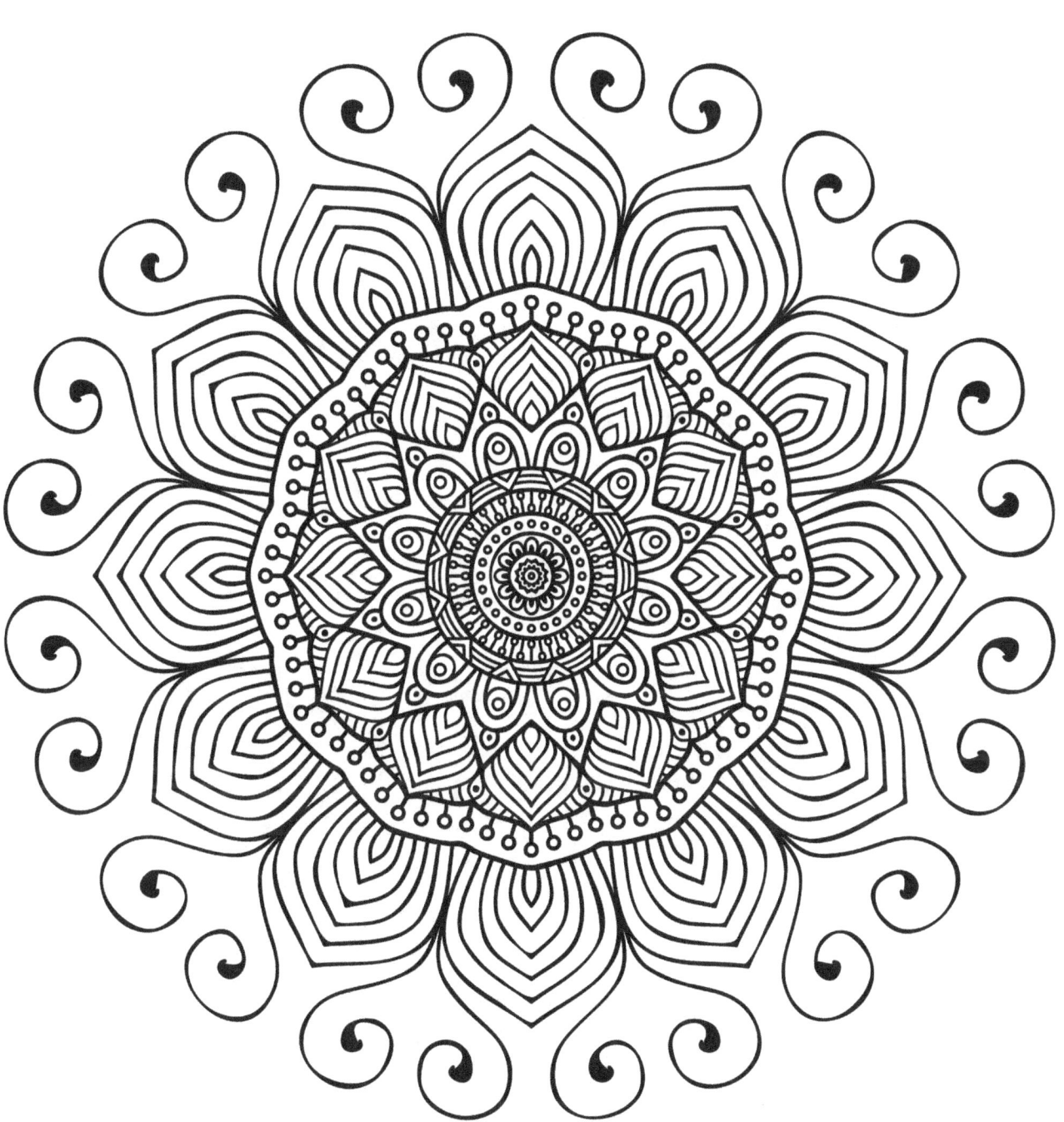

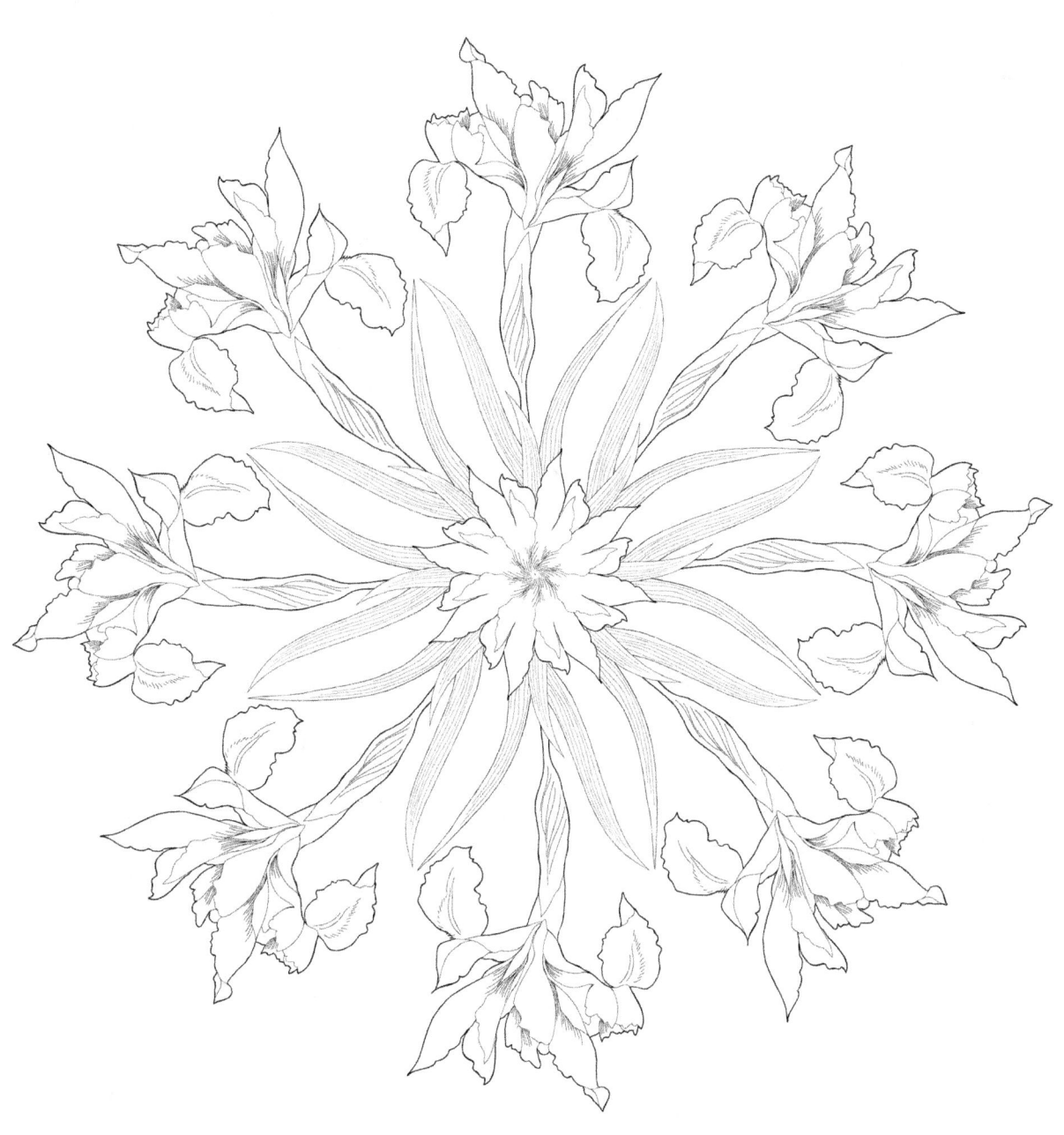

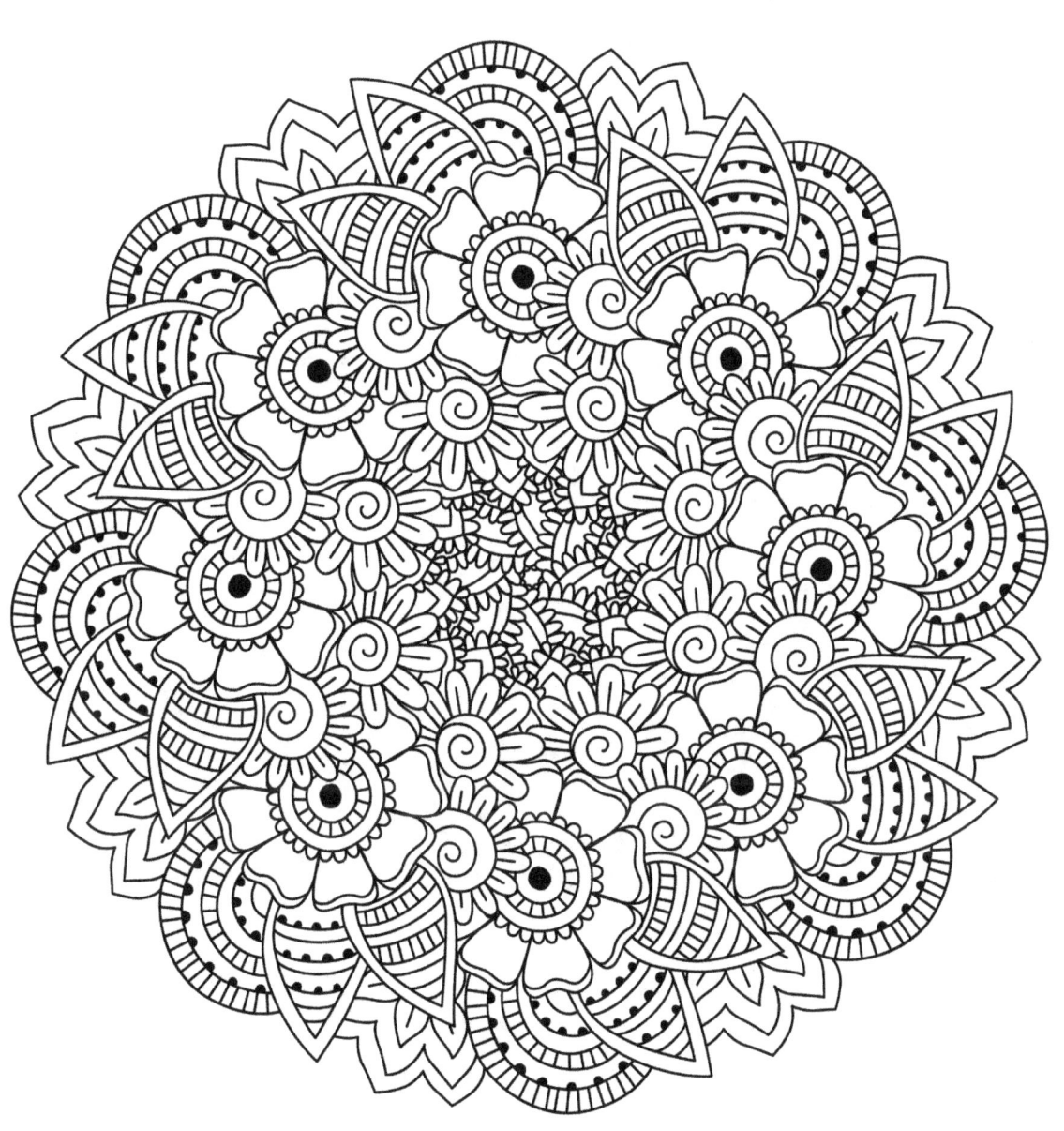

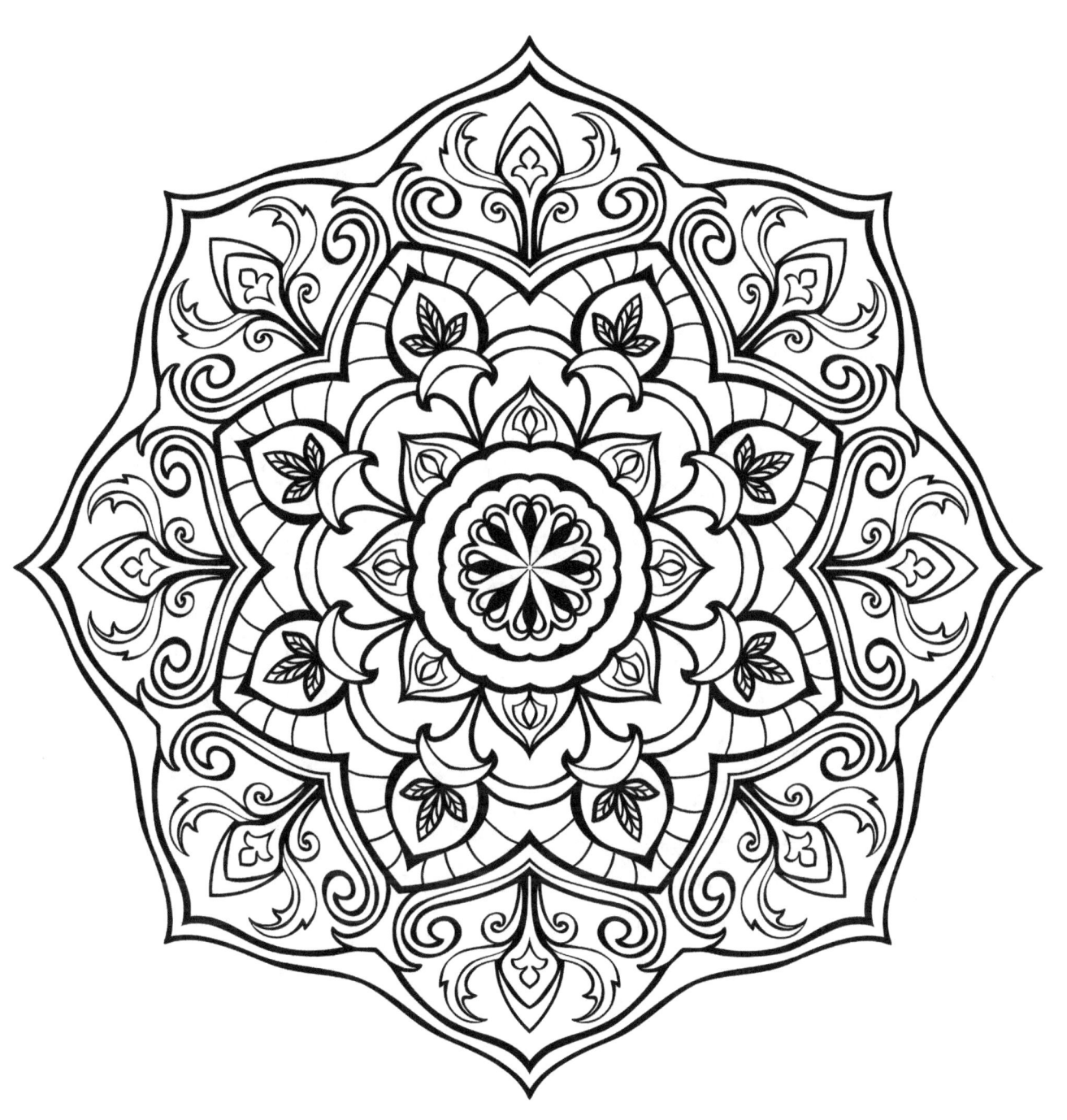

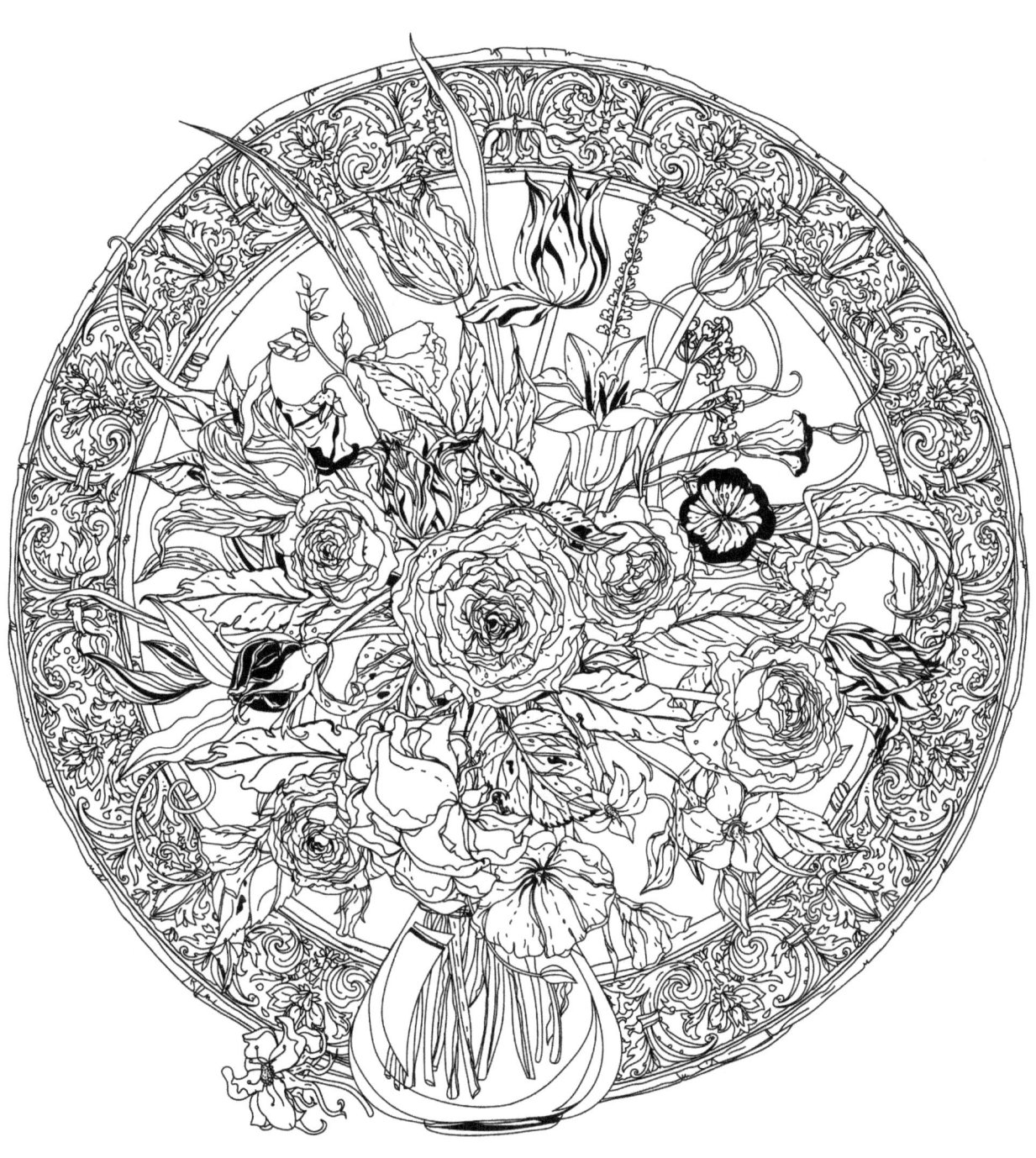

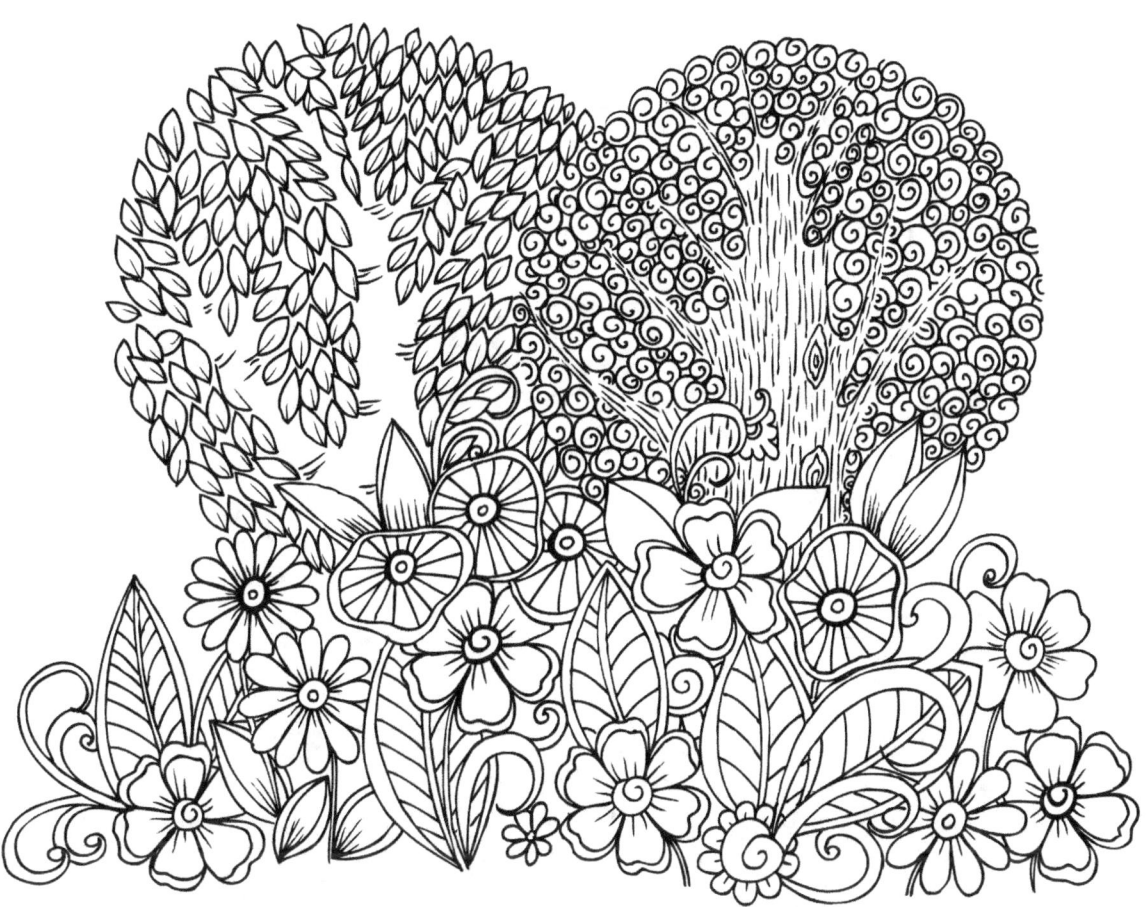

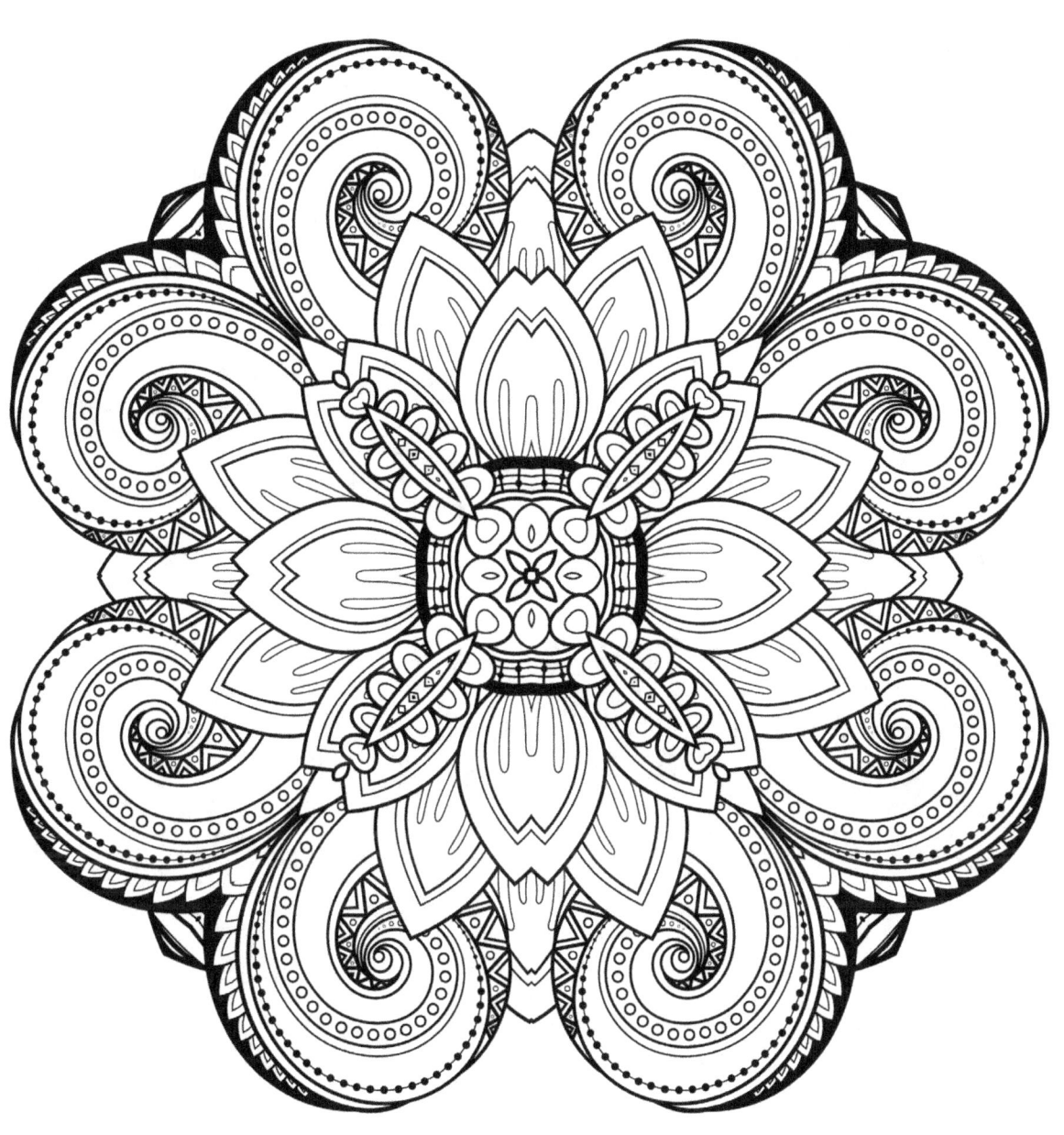

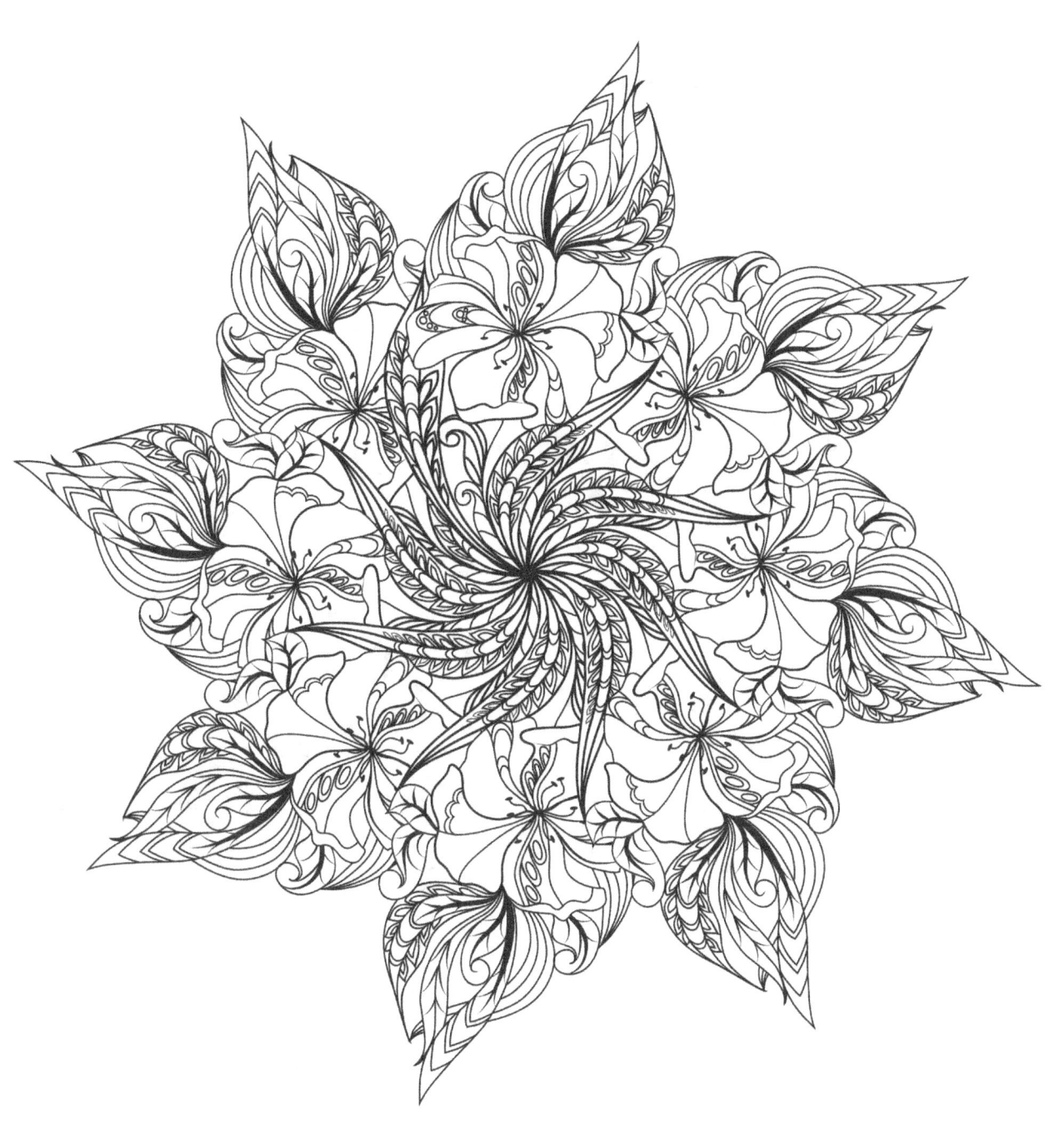

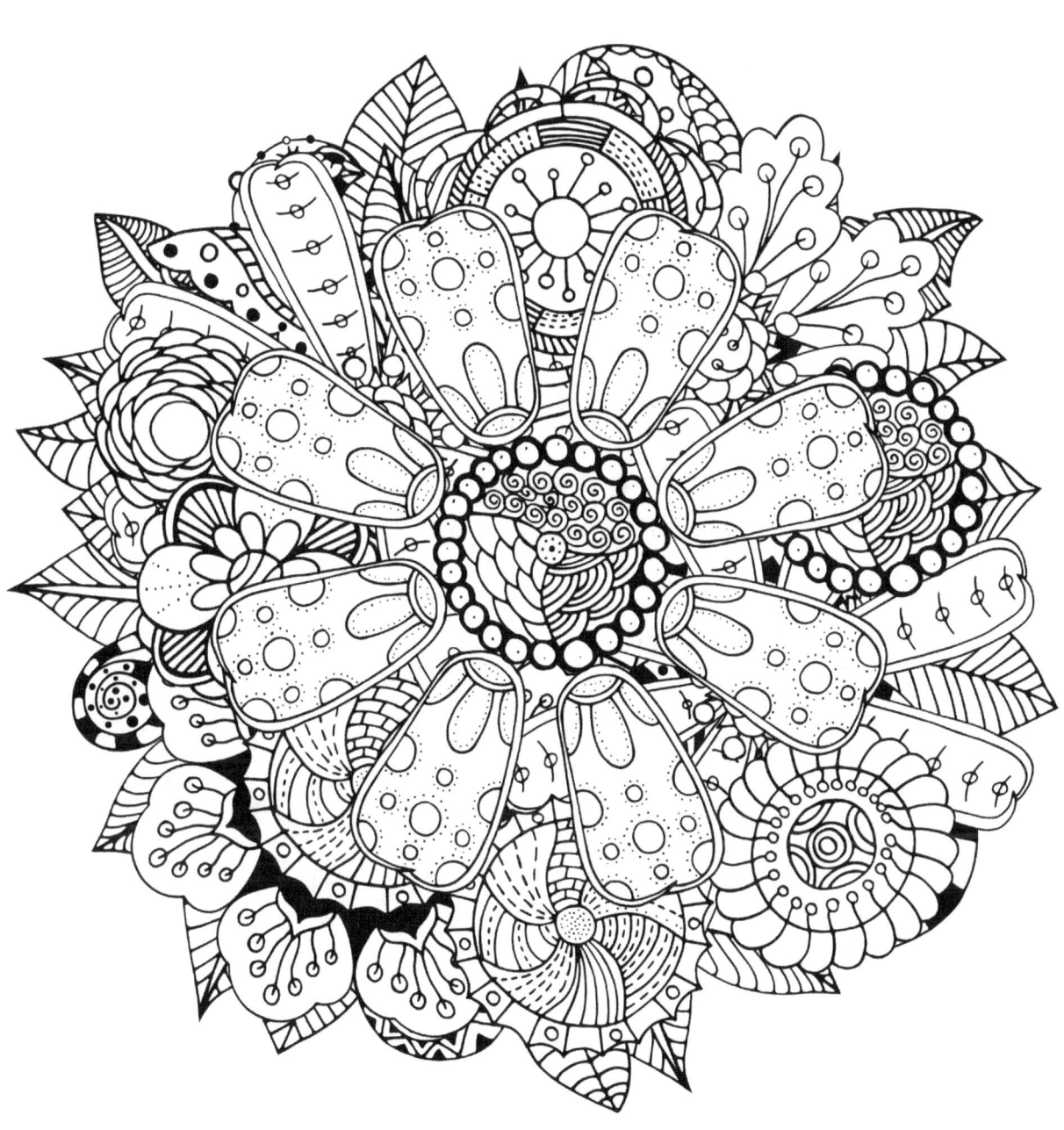

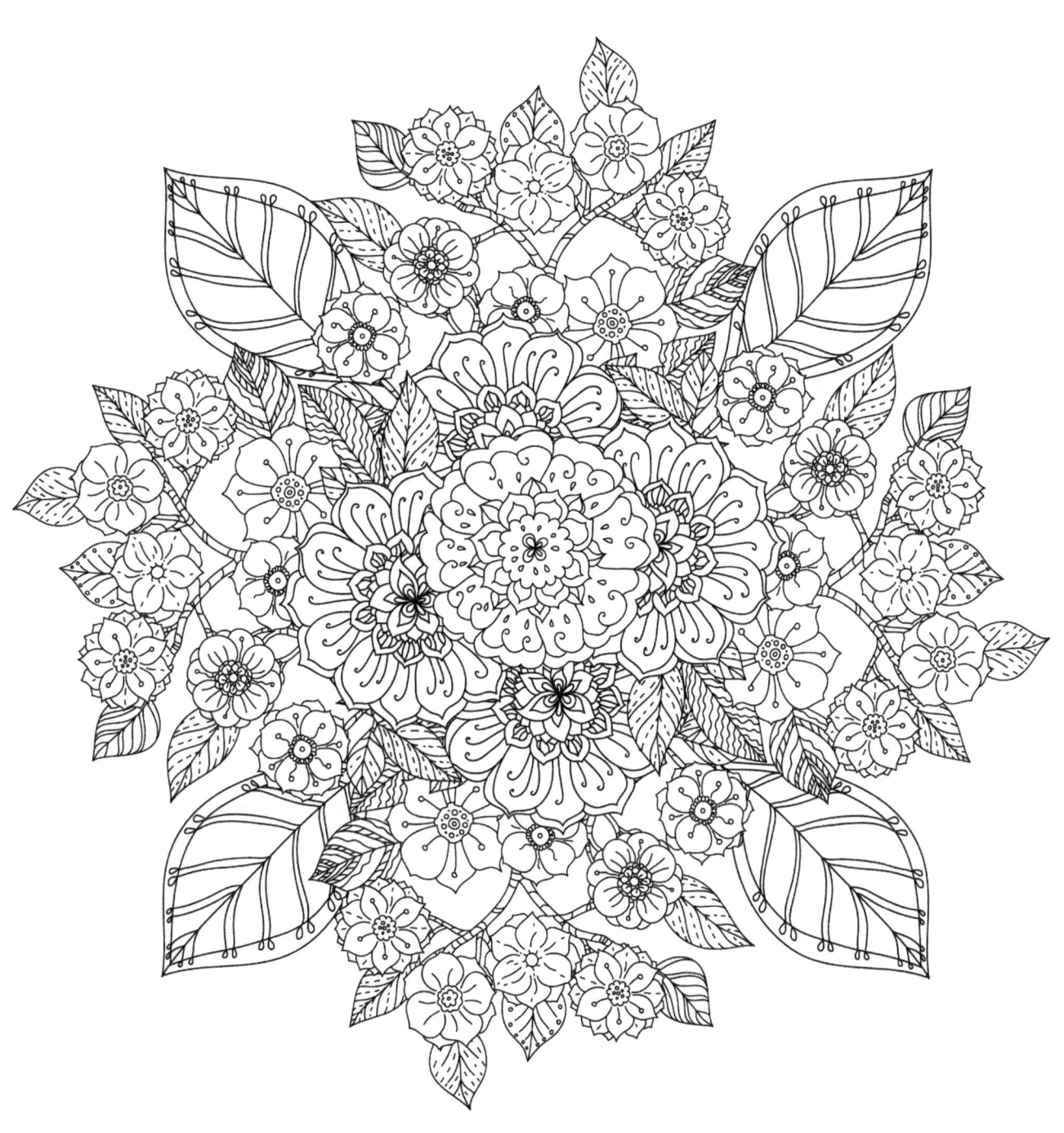

www.ingramcontent.com/pod-product-compliance
Lightning Source LLC
Chambersburg PA
CBHW060014210526
45170CB00018B/2940